COLD ★ WAR
TEXAS

COLD ★ WAR
TEXAS

LANDRY BREWER

FOREWORD BY AMANDA BILES

THE
History
PRESS

Published by The History Press
Charleston, SC
www.historypress.com

Copyright © 2022 by Landry Brewer
All rights reserved

First published 2022

Manufactured in the United States

ISBN 9781467152471

Library of Congress Control Number: 2022936208

For Erin, Dylan, Kelsey, MacKinley, Quinn and Spence.

CONTENTS

Foreword, by Amanda Biles   9
Acknowledgements   11
Introduction   13

1. Cold War Origins   17
2. Texas Missiles   23
3. Lone Star State Civil Defense   60
4. Texas Military Installations   88
5. Pantex: Nuclear Stockpile Guarantor   114
6. Maurice Halperin: Texas-Oklahoma Communist, Soviet Spy   119
7. Cold War Legacy   133

Notes   137
About the Author   155

FOREWORD

This latest book in Professor Landry Brewer's state-by-state Cold War series brings to life the vivid experiences of Texans who did their part to stand against the Soviet Empire from right here in the Lone Star State. Much of this legacy lies hidden now; the missile silos that slumber mere miles from my city are flooded and overgrown. Some weapon systems—like the nuclear-capable Nike Hercules surface-to-air missile—are not only gone; they are largely forgotten. This is a story worth telling.

Brewer ably demonstrates that when the Cold War came to Texas, her citizens rallied to support the American cause. They welcomed new military bases with expanded missions, established civil defense efforts for their own protection and embodied the practical, do-it-yourself attitude that Texans are known for—even when it came to fixing broken missile silo doors.

Professor Brewer's research takes his reader through the entire Texas Cold War experience, from origins to early nuclear buildup, then through civil defense and even espionage. He tells of universities, schools and civic organizations banding together to provide shelter from possible fallout. He examines the work of leading Texans like Sam Rayburn and Lyndon Johnson, the first rallying support for international aid and the second calming the fears of a fractured Berlin. He provides needed insight on the relationship between cities and their nuclear neighbors.

As a Texan, a historian and a military spouse (who has spent many years married to the nuclear mission), I particularly appreciate this coverage of the role Texas played in developing the United States nuclear arsenal. Texas built, housed and deployed both long-range nuclear bombers and ICBMs in the fight against the Soviet Union. She hosted two legs of the nuclear triad and assembled the warheads for the third—the nuclear submarines and their submarine-launched ballistic missile payloads.

These efforts left a lasting impact on Texas communities. Her citizens knew they would likely be caught in the crosshairs of any Soviet attack, and they responded to this danger with Texas-sized resolve. Their stories are all chronicled here, in another excellent installment of our nation's Cold War history.

—Amanda B. Biles, PhD

Amanda Biles is assistant professor of history and director of the public history program at Abilene Christian University in Abilene, Texas.

ACKNOWLEDGEMENTS

I owe a debt of gratitude to The History Press for publishing this book. Thank you for seeing the value in it.

Acquisitions editor Ben Gibson once again showed great patience and was extremely pleasant to work with on this book.

The SWOSU administration and my colleagues there continue to support my research and writing.

Despite their weariness with my talk of missiles, fallout shelters and all things Cold War, my family remains a source of inspiration.

INTRODUCTION*

The Cold War was frightening. For more than four decades, Americans feared that civilization would melt in the fervent heat of a nuclear exchange if the Cold War between the United States and the Soviet Union got hot. And Texans knew that if the Soviet Union launched a nuclear attack, they would likely be targeted.

After victory in World War II, the United States found itself the leader of the Free World. The Soviet Union's Red Army had marched into Eastern Europe en route to Berlin to force a Nazi surrender. Where the Red Army went, Communism usually followed. Millions of Poles, Germans, Czechs and others found themselves enslaved under Communist rule, puppet states controlled by Moscow.

In the mind of many Americans, Joseph Stalin had replaced Adolf Hitler as the dictator trying to conquer Europe and the world. Because no other nation had the ability to intervene and stop Soviet expansion, American foreign policy in the late 1940s changed with the intent of stopping Communism's march. In 1947, President Truman announced that the United States would stop Communism's attempt to undermine and control free people with economic, political and, if necessary, military assistance. The latter included the atomic bomb.

The nation—including Texas—readied itself for what President Kennedy later called a "long twilight struggle."

A version of this chapter previously appeared in Landry Brewer, Cold War Oklahoma (Charleston, SC: The History Press, 2019).

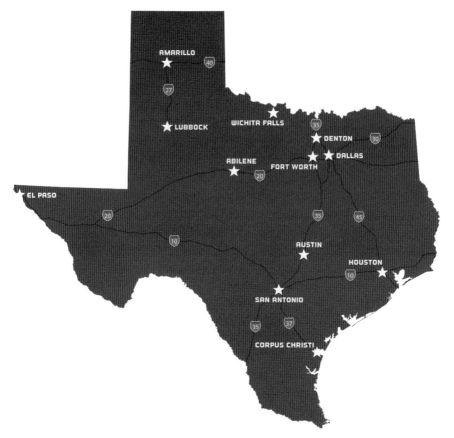

Texas map locating twelve of the cities featured prominently in state Cold War activities. *Southwestern Oklahoma State University. Graphics designer: Kyle Wright.*

From all over the state, Texans joined national efforts to bolster national security and stop Communism because the Soviet Union appeared intent on conquering our European allies and further spreading its influence. With its acquiring thermonuclear weapons and the ability to deliver them, that nation also appeared intent on attacking the United States and inflicting possibly civilization-ending destruction.

Texans from all walks of life sprang into action. Some military bases in the state were opened and others were expanded. Long-range missile sites were built and operated; so were antiaircraft missile sites. Civilians prepared to survive the effects of a nuclear attack. State and national politicians from Texas readied their governments to protect their constituents and preserve the nation's way of life in the face of grave—and at times imminent—danger.

The Cold War was dangerous. For the world. For the nation. For Texas.

This books tells an important story. It reminds us that the world became extremely dangerous and remained so for more than four decades when nations with nuclear weapons at their disposal came close to using them against each other.

And it reminds us of Texas's important role then.

In a 1961 speech to the United Nations, during the Cold War's most dangerous era, President Kennedy said, "Every man, woman and child lives under a nuclear sword of Damocles, hanging by the slenderest of threads, capable of being cut at any moment by accident or miscalculation or by madness."[1]

Texans did what they could to keep family members, friends, neighbors and constituents safe. They built missile sites and lived with nuclear-armed missiles. They taught citizens how to install fallout shelters. They served in the military. They served in the government. For forty-five years, Texans fought the long twilight struggle, hoping the sword of Damocles would never fall.

The four-plus decades of danger were, perhaps, more tangible for Texas than they were for much of the nation. This book explains why. This book tells Texas's Cold War story.

CHAPTER 1

COLD WAR ORIGINS†

Though the United States and the Soviet Union were allies during World War II, the two nations became adversaries when the war ended in 1945. The Nazi military had taken control of Eastern Europe by the end of 1941. When the war ended four years later, the Red Army, having defeated the German army on its march to Berlin, controlled that territory for the Soviet Union. "The Soviet Union occupied East Europe. This crucial result of World War II destroyed the Grand Alliance and gave birth to the Cold War," according to historians Stephen Ambrose and Douglas Brinkley.[2]

At the February 1945 Yalta Conference three months before World War II ended in Europe with Germany's surrender, leaders of the United States, Great Britain and the Soviet Union—Franklin Roosevelt, Winston Churchill and Joseph Stalin, respectively—agreed to postwar arrangements in Europe. In return for the Soviet Union's joining the war against Japan within three months of Germany's surrender, Roosevelt and Churchill consented to allow the Soviet Union to exert control over Eastern Europe—but only if Stalin promised to allow free elections there. Stalin agreed. However, according to Ambrose and Brinkley, Stalin "never accepted the Western interpretation of the Yalta agreements." The Soviet Union controlled Eastern Europe and did not intend to relinquish that control.[3]

The United States dropped two atomic bombs on the Japanese cities Hiroshima and Nagasaki in August 1945. Shortly thereafter the Japanese

---

† *A version of this chapter previously appeared in Brewer,* Cold War Oklahoma.

government surrendered, and World War II ended. As conditions between the former war allies worsened and the Soviet Union consolidated control over much of Europe, former British prime minister Churchill played the role of prophet when he delivered a March 5, 1946 speech in President Truman's home state at Westminster College in Fulton, Missouri, with the president seated nearby. In what is now known as the iron curtain speech, Churchill said this about Soviet control of the eastern portion of a divided Europe:

> *From Stettin in the Baltic to Trieste in the Adriatic an "iron curtain" has descended across the continent. Behind that line lie all the capitals of the ancient states of Central and Eastern Europe. Warsaw, Berlin, Prague, Vienna, Budapest, Belgrade, Bucharest and Sofia; all these famous cities and the populations around them lie in what I must call the Soviet sphere, and all are subject, in one form or another, not only to Soviet influence but to a very high and in some cases increasing measure of control from Moscow.*[4]

By 1947, President Truman's foreign policy toward the Soviet Union and Communism was intensifying. State Department official William C. Bullitt gave a mid-1947 speech at the National War College in which he likened Stalin to Hitler and said that the Soviet Union wanted to conquer the world. Communists threatened to replace the British-supported Greek government, though British aid and forty thousand British troops in Greece were preventing that from happening. When the British government informed the Americans in February 1947 that no further aid would be forthcoming and British troops would soon return home, President Truman decided that the United States must intervene. He believed that if Greece fell to Communism, its neighbor Turkey, which had been pressured by the Soviet Union to allow it a military presence there, would be next to fall. On March 12, 1947, President Truman addressed a joint session of Congress, appealing for American aid for both countries and announcing the Truman Doctrine: "I believe that it must be the policy of the United States to support free peoples who are resisting attempted subjugation by armed minorities or by outside pressures."[5]

Congress granted Truman's request with $400 million in aid for Greece and Turkey, and the United States began a new era, described this way by Ambrose and Brinkley: "For the first time in its history, the United States had chosen to intervene during a period of general peace in the affairs of peoples outside North and South America." President Truman had articulated the

American government's new policy of containment, through which the nation sought to stop the spread of Soviet Communism.[6]

According to Truman biographer David McCullough, American policy toward the Soviet Union changed markedly after Secretary of State George Marshall returned from a 1947 meeting with his European counterparts. Marshall told Truman that the United States could not deal with the Soviets and diplomacy was destined to fail. By late 1947, the conflict between the United States and the Soviet Union was being called the Cold War by columnist Walter Lippman. Though the expression had been used earlier, Lippmann was the first to attach it to the increasingly hostile East-West divide.[7]

Secretary Marshall returned on Saturday, April 26, 1947, shocked by what he had seen in Berlin and Western Europe during his trip, which included a visit to Moscow for talks with the Soviet government. Slow to recover economically from the ravages of World War II, Western Europe was teetering on the brink of economic collapse and needed to be rescued. Marshall instructed his State Department to formulate a plan to give economic aid that would help revive Europe's economy. "Millions of people were slowly starving. A collapse in Europe would mean revolution and a tailspin for the American economy."[8] Marshall announced what was officially the European Recovery Program, which came to be called the Marshall Plan—its goal to help prevent economic collapse and starvation, ensure that the United States had economically viable trading partners in Europe and stave off a Communist takeover of Western Europe—in a June 5 speech at Harvard, in which he declared the plan's intent:

> *Our policy is directed not against any country or doctrine, but against hunger, poverty, desperation and chaos. Its purpose should be the revival of a working economy in the world so as to permit the emergence of political and social conditions in which free institutions can exist.*[9]

The amount requested for Marshall Plan aid to Europe was $17 billion, and fearing Congress would refuse to appropriate the money, President Truman met with Speaker of the House Sam Rayburn to sell the idea. "Truman said there was no way of telling how many hundreds of thousands of people would starve to death in Europe and that this must not happen, not if it could be prevented." Truman "was also sure…that if Europe went 'down the drain' in a depression, the United States would follow." He said to the speaker that they had "both lived through one depression, and we don't want to have to live through another one, do we, Sam?" The Marshall Plan was passed by Congress almost one year after Marshall's Harvard speech, in April 1948.[10]

Also important for American Cold War military operations and foreign policy was passage by Congress of the National Security Act of 1947. President Truman sent the bill to Congress for its consideration in February. The purpose of the bill was to reorganize the nation's military so that its several branches were all brought under the oversight of the newly created Department of Defense (DOD), headed by a secretary of defense. In addition to creating the DOD, the legislation also created a separate air force, removing it from the army. The National Security Act also created the National Security Council and the Central Intelligence Agency.[11]

The eastern portion of Berlin had been occupied by the Soviets with the Americans, British and French in the western portion of the city since World War II ended, each country within its own sector. In the summer of 1948, Joseph Stalin ordered a blockade of Berlin to prevent the Western powers from gaining access to the city by ground or water transport, in an attempt to starve the democracies into submission and force them out of the city. Opinions within the American government differed as to what the country's response should be, though President Truman was adamant that the United States stand its ground. Army chief of staff Omar Bradley informed President Truman that access to West Berlin could be gained by air. According to scholar Richard Reeves, soon, "air transport...flying round-the-clock missions into Berlin, supplying up to 13,000 tons of goods per day" commenced, and "[t]he Berlin airlift caught the imagination of the world."[12] The airlift lasted just under one year before Stalin finally lifted the blockade in 1949, and per Reeves,

> *Official U.S. Air Force numbers include*[d]*: total cargo delivered to Berlin—2,325,809 tons, 1,783,573 of those by the Air Force and 542,236 tons by the Royal Air Forces of Britain, Australia and New Zealand, along with private aircraft chartered by the British government. The total number of flights into Berlin was recorded as 277,569—189,963 by the Americans, and 87,606 by the British and their Commonwealth partners.*[13]

The triumph of the Berlin airlift overlapped with another diplomatic triumph: the creation of the North Atlantic Treaty Organization (NATO). Delivering his inaugural address after winning the 1948 presidential election, Truman "pledged...to aid those European nations willing to defend themselves." Carrying out the president's wishes, Secretary of State Dean

Acheson brokered the North Atlantic Treaty, which was signed on April 4, 1949, in Washington, D.C. The United States, Canada, Great Britain, France and several other Western European nations promised to defend each other if any member was attacked.[14] NATO was born, furthering the cause of containment in Europe.

Any feelings of triumph were overwhelmed by concern as summer became fall in 1949. In early September, an Air Force plane discovered radioactivity over the northern Pacific Ocean. On Monday, September 19, the scientists who reviewed the radioactive samples that had been gathered concluded that the Soviet Union had, for the first time, detonated an atomic bomb. The American atomic monopoly had ended. President Truman was informed the next day. He released a statement to the press on Friday, September 23, informing the American public, and according to Truman biographer David McCullough, "Though there was no panic in the country, the fears and tensions of the Cold War were greatly amplified. It was a different world now."[15]

Early the next month, the years-long Chinese civil war fought between Communists led by Mao Tse-tung and Nationalists led by American ally Chiang Kai-shek came to an end. Although the United States had spent billions of dollars supporting Chiang in hopes of staving off Communism's advances in China since World War II ended, it was not enough. In McCullough's words, just one week after President Truman informed the American people that the Soviet Union had acquired its own atomic bomb, "the People's Republic of China, the most numerous Communist nation in the world, with more than 500 million people, one fifth of humanity, was officially inaugurated."[16]

That same month, October 1949, the Cold War intensified yet again. Soon after President Truman informed the nation that the Soviets had the atomic bomb, American officials began to discuss pursuing "a thermonuclear or hydrogen weapon—a superbomb, or 'Super'—which would have more than ten times the destructive power of the bombs dropped on Hiroshima and Nagasaki." The belief was that if the Soviets had the capacity to build an atomic bomb, they would likely have the means and desire to create their own thermonuclear bomb, which meant that the United States must also have this weapon. President Truman agreed with his advisors who followed this logic, and on January 31, 1950, he officially signed off on developing the hydrogen—or thermonuclear—bomb.[17]

Because of Communist ascendancy in China, the Soviet acquisition of the atomic bomb and the specter of a Soviet thermonuclear bomb—and the domestic political pressure that these events created—on January 30, 1950, President Truman tasked the Department of State and the Department of Defense with reviewing the nation's defense and foreign policy. A report was prepared, forwarded to the National Security Council, then delivered to the president as National Security Council Paper No. 68. NSC 68 advocated a massive military buildup in an effort to offset Communist gains and discourage further Soviet expansion. It predicted that "the Soviets would probably achieve nuclear equality by 1954," and although the document did not specify costs, President Truman was told that spending between $40 and $50 billion a year—triple the existing defense budget—would likely be necessary. The report ended ominously by telling President Truman, "'The whole success hangs ultimately on recognition by this government, the American people and all the peoples that the Cold War is in fact a real war in which the survival of the world is at stake."[18]

That summer, Communist North Korean troops invaded South Korea. The United States would fight a three-year war trying to restore the antebellum status quo and prevent a Communist takeover of the southern half of the Korean Peninsula. Then, in the 1960s, Americans began fighting another war, itself a decade-long conflict in Southeast Asia to prevent a Communist takeover in South Vietnam. Between the two Cold War–inspired hot conflicts, the United States and the Soviet Union would reach the brink of nuclear war, each with long-range bombers and ballistic missiles that could fly thousands of miles with nuclear bombs capable of inflicting civilization-ending destruction. Then, as the 1970s became the 1980s, the nuclear arms race between the United States and the Soviet Union resumed, and new fears of nuclear war emerged. Throughout these decades, Americans—including Texans—hoped for the best but prepared for the worst. The Cold War ushered in a different world, indeed.

CHAPTER 2

TEXAS MISSILES

As the Soviet Union appeared to surpass American nuclear capability in the late 1950s, the United States government moved quickly to reassert its nuclear dominance. That nuclear dominance was on display in the early 1960s in Texas, as several locations near Dyess Air Force Base (AFB) in Abilene operated intercontinental ballistic missiles (ICBMs) as part of the nation's offensive nuclear arsenal. Additionally, the state operated defensive antiaircraft missile sites to protect some of the state's most important cities against possible attack. Housing those missiles required massive construction projects that provided thousands of individuals with jobs and infused the state with large sums of money, which was welcomed by many Texans, who learned to live with nuclear weapons in their midst. Most importantly, those ICBMs fortified the nation's nuclear deterrent, and antiaircraft missiles defended Americans during the Cold War's most dangerous years.

ATLAS

During Dwight Eisenhower's presidency (1953–61), American defense policy relied heavily on the nation's nuclear arsenal deterring Soviet aggression against the United States or its allies. President Eisenhower assumed office wanting to spend less money than his predecessor on national defense by reducing conventional forces and their costs. Instead, Eisenhower believed that the nation could get more for its money while maintaining its security by responding to Soviet threats against the United States and its allies with threats of nuclear retaliation. Called the New Look by the administration and massive retaliation by the media, Eisenhower's policy of nuclear deterrence relied on American nuclear superiority.[19]

Central to this deterrence was development of ICBMs. The nation's first ICBM was the Atlas. Development of the Atlas missile had begun by the mid-1950s, but things changed dramatically when the Soviet Union announced that it had successfully launched the world's first ICBM in September 1957, then launched the Sputnik satellite just one month later. Pressure quickly mounted on the American government to complete the Atlas project. The Cold War power balance had shifted dramatically in 1949 when the Soviet Union acquired an atomic bomb, and the power balance appeared to shift dramatically again eight years later. The United States scrambled to right the perceived imbalance.[20]

Convair Astronautics, later made a division of General Dynamics, began work on the Atlas in the early 1950s. Though only ten employees were assigned to the ballistic missile project in 1953, twelve thousand employees worked on the Atlas program in the company's San Diego facility in 1960. "Reflecting the truly national scope of the Atlas program," wrote John C. Lonnquest and David F. Winkler in the Department of Defense document *To Defend and Deter: The Legacy of the United States Cold War Missile Program*, "Convair employed 30 major subcontractors, 500 lesser contractors, and 5,000 suppliers scattered across 32 states."[21]

Six versions of the Atlas missile were produced—the A, B and C were test models, and the D, E and F were deployed and operational. The Atlas missile was 82.5 feet long and 10 feet wide and weighed 18,104 pounds empty and 267,136 pounds when filled with liquid fuel. In flight, the missile reached speeds of sixteen thousand miles per hour, allowing it to travel nearly seven thousand miles in just 43 minutes, landing within two nautical miles of its target. Upon arrival, the Atlas's warhead would deliver a four-megaton yield. To put this into perspective, each Atlas missile in Texas would have delivered a nuclear bomb more than 255 times more powerful than the atomic bomb dropped by the United States on Hiroshima and more than 182 times more powerful than the atomic bomb dropped on Nagasaki in August 1945 at the end of World War II.[22]

The air force used several criteria to determine the locations of ICBM launch sites. Each location had to be within the continental United States, close enough for the missile to reach its intended target but also outside the range of Soviet missiles launched from submarines. Finally, the air force secretary ordered that, if possible, launch sites be on government property, ideally in an area with a population of at least fifty thousand. Believing that the launch sites would be targeted by the Soviet Union in the event of war, they were placed with sufficient distance between each to prevent multiple installations from being disrupted by a single Soviet bomb.[23]

The air force used the U.S. Army Corps of Engineers to build the launch complexes. The Corps of Engineers tasked nearby engineer districts with construction. The job proved difficult because of the immediate and intense nature of the program, especially after the fall of 1957 when the ICBM program was accelerated. The air force increased the number of Atlas squadrons that it would deploy. Even though the launch sites became more complex, making them increasingly difficult and costly to build, they were, however, to be built as quickly as possible. Adding to these difficulties was the method used by the air force known as the concept of concurrency—ICBMs were being developed and tested while the Corps of Engineers simultaneously built the missile launch complexes. An air force missile design change could require the Corps of Engineers to change the missile sites they were building, including destroying and removing what had just been built and starting anew. By April 1962, the Army Corps of Engineers had approved more than 2,600 Atlas launch-site modifications during construction. These modifications cost an additional $96 million, which was 40 percent more than the initial contract amount. Because of the perceived need to deploy ICBMs as quickly as possible, deployment speed trumped cost, and the concurrency method was used.[24]

The most sophisticated among the Atlas missiles, the Atlas F was created to be housed in deep, "hardened" underground silos to protect them against possible Soviet nuclear attack. Constructed of the strongest concrete possible, each silo was 174 feet deep with a diameter of 52 feet, and each was entirely below ground. Each silo housed a missile along with an extensive steel structure, the "crib"—attached to the silo walls by four extremely large springs—that allowed for routine missile maintenance. Connected to the silo by a 50-foot-long, 8-foot-wide tunnel was the launch control center. Also built of reinforced concrete, the underground structure housed the equipment to fire the missile; the missile would be raised with an elevator through the silo top, then launched. Of all the Atlas missile sites, the F series were the most difficult and expensive to build.[25]

To oversee the mammoth task of building several ICBM sites around the nation, the army created the Corps of Engineers Ballistic Missile Construction Office, or CEBMCO, in August 1960. One of CEBMCO's goals was to

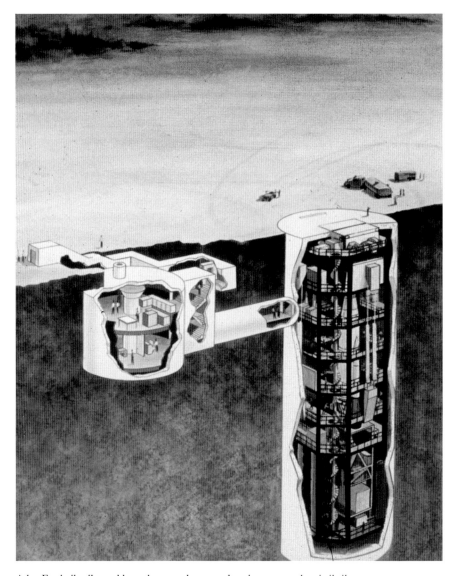

Atlas F missile silo and launch control center drawing. *www.atlasmissilesilo.com.*

provide continuity and consistency through centralized control in building missile sites. According to Lonnquest and Winkler, "To do that, CEBMCO's commanding officer appointed weapon system directors for the Atlas F… facility construction programs," which was done "through a network of CEBMCO area offices, one of which was located at each major site" and which oversaw construction. The Corps of Engineers Dyess Area Office was activated on April 18, 1960, under the oversight of the Fort Worth U.S. Army Engineer District, under District Engineer Colonel Walter J. Wells. Lieutenant Colonel Albert M. Antonelli became acting area engineer as commander for the office the following week; then, on June 27, 1960, Antonelli's title changed to area engineer. He remained commander of the Dyess Area Office throughout construction of the twelve Atlas F missile launch sites. Though the Dyess Area Office was made a part of CEBMCO, headquartered in Los Angeles, California, on December 1, 1960, the Fort Worth U.S. Army Engineer District administratively supported the project under CEBMCO's oversight.[26]

The missiles at the Dyess AFB Atlas F sites, along with those at Lincoln AFB in Nebraska, Altus AFB in Oklahoma, Schilling AFB in Kansas, Walker AFB in New Mexico and Plattsburg AFB in New York, were the nation's first to be maintained entirely underground in large, protective silos. Each air force base had twelve missile sites attached to it, and they were usually spaced less than forty miles from each other. The large vertical Atlas F silos were built to withstand overpressures reaching 100 psi. Lonnquest and Winkler provide this explanation of overpressure:

> *The normal atmospheric pressure at sea level is 15 psi. Overpressure is an additional, transient pressure created by the shock or blast wave following a powerful explosion. Buildings collapse at 6 psi overpressure. Humans can withstand up to 30 psi overpressure, but a level over 5 psi can rupture eardrums and cause internal hemorrhaging.*[27]

Each Atlas F missile rested vertically inside a silo made of heavily reinforced concrete, the top of which was 9 feet thick, tapering downward 174 feet to the bottom, where the wall was 2.5 feet thick. The silo's diameter was 52 feet. The crib inside each silo, made of 389 tons of heavy steel, was suspended from the silo's wall by extremely heavy rods attached to four devices called shock hangars. Two diesel generators, equipment to collect dust, air conditioners and electrical and mechanical equipment were also installed in each silo. A propellant loading system was also installed in each silo to fuel the missile and ready it for firing. Each launch complex included a two-floor launch control center, or LCC, which was also located underground and built of heavily reinforced concrete. The electronic equipment to fire the missile was located inside each LCC. A water treatment building and a cooling tower, an interior security fence and a perimeter fence, a paved road from the nearby highway to the site, sewage disposal and lighting were also installed at each missile site.[28]

The Fort Worth U.S. Army Engineer District advertised the construction contract for the twelve Dyess AFB missile launch sites on April 29, 1960, and six bids were submitted. These six were opened the following May 26 at Abilene, and the winning low bid was a joint bid by H.B. Zachry Company and Brown and Root Inc. of $20,075,000. Because of construction modifications, that amount rose to $30,558,784.82.[29] The Brown and Root construction firm's owners, Herman and George Brown, were large campaign contributors to Lyndon B. Johnson from his earliest days in the U.S. House of Representatives. The Browns benefited greatly from their association with Johnson throughout his political career, including his presidency, when Houston's Brown and Root was the foremost contractor that built American military bases in Vietnam. In fact, according to Johnson biographer Charles Peters, "Brown & Root would become expert at using 'change orders' that permitted the firm to run up costs beyond the bids that had won its contracts" and would continue doing so even through the Iraq War in the early 2000s as the Halliburton subsidiary Kellogg, Brown & Root.[30]

Construction of Dyess Air Force Base–area Atlas F missile launch site in the early 1960s. *Defense Visual Information Distribution Service.*

This page: Construction of Albany Atlas F missile launch site in the early 1960s. *Defense Visual Information Distribution Service.*

This page and opposite: Construction of Dyess Air Force Base–area Atlas F missile launch site in the early 1960s. *Defense Visual Information Distribution Service.*

The twelve sites chosen for Atlas F launch complexes were Baird, Denton, Oplin, Lawn, Bradshaw, Winters, Shep, Nolan, Anson, Phantom Lake, Albany and Corinth West. A story in the July 1, 1960 edition of the *Winters Enterprise* about that site's construction referenced H.B. Zachry Company and Brown and Root, Inc. project manager D.V. Moore, who said that "the first, or open excavation, will be completed within ten days, and then work on the excavation for the deep shaft for the Atlas silo will begin." The story described the "surface excavation" as "about the size of a football field,

sloping to a depth of about 40 feet in diameter and 180 feet deep." Project construction began with excavation at the Baird site on June 6, 1960.[31]

Building ICBM launch sites was dangerous; nationally, more than fifty people died in silo accidents.[32] This included four deaths during construction of the Dyess-area sites. The first fatality occurred at the Oplin site about ten thirty in the morning on April 2, 1961, when James C. Chandler, a Convair-Astronautics plant engineer, stepped backward while working on the silo top, lost his footing and fell 174 feet to the silo's cement bottom. Chandler was taken to Abilene's Hendrick Memorial Hospital, where he was pronounced dead. Chandler's family had moved from Fort Worth to Abilene in the fall of 1960 when he began working on the missile sites project.[33]

Two weeks later, the April 17, 1961 edition of the *Abilene Reporter-News* carried word of the Bay of Pigs invasion in Cuba, the failed U.S.-backed plan for Cuban exiles to overthrow communist dictator Fidel Castro. A page 1 Associated Press story referred to the invasion as "the long-awaited battle to topple Fidel Castro." Castro publicly blamed the United States for supporting the invaders, and other Cuban government officials even charged that the invaders came from Florida and Guatemala. The story referenced the Soviet newspaper *Izvestia*'s declaration that the Soviet Union and all Communist countries supported Castro, and the story also alluded to a promise by Soviet leader Nikita Khrushchev the previous summer to defend Cuba, with missiles if necessary.[34]

The next day's Abilene newspaper printed more invasion stories under the banner headline "Khrushchev Asks U.S. to Halt Rebel Invasion." An Associated Press story relayed that Khrushchev, speaking through the Soviet *Tass* news agency, called on President Kennedy to stop the invasion, warning that "any so-called 'small war' can produce a chain reaction in all parts of the world." After accusing the United States of training and arming the invaders, Khrushchev said that the American government must stop the fighting from "spreading into a conflagration which it will be impossible to cope with" and that the American-supported invasion of their Cuban Communist comrades' country "arouses the understandable indignation of the Soviet government, the Soviet people." Eighteen months later, the Abilene-area missiles would have a prominent role in another Cuban crisis, this one involving Soviet missiles.[35]

When President John F. Kennedy entered the White House in January 1961, he was determined to change national defense policy. During the 1960 presidential campaign, Kennedy had been critical of the Eisenhower administration's "massive retaliation" approach, and upon assuming office,

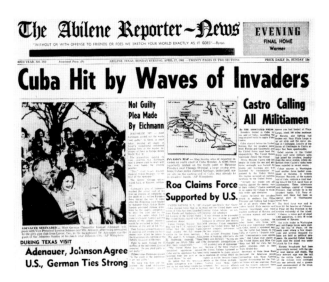

Front page of the
April 17, 1961
Abilene Reporter-News.
newspaperarchive.com.

he implemented a "Flexible Response" policy, allowing for a range of military options against enemy aggression that included nonnuclear actions.[36] Kennedy continued to expand the nation's nuclear capabilities, though. In President Eisenhower's final year in office in 1960, the United States had twelve ICBMs and approximately 1,500 long-range bombers.[37] In March 1961, President Kennedy wanted to expand the defense budget to increase the stockpile of ICBMs, the number of Polaris submarines that carried nuclear missiles aimed at the Soviet Union and the number of B-52 bombers on constant alert.[38] Two months later, in a special message to Congress, President Kennedy spoke of the need to maintain a nuclear arsenal of such overwhelming force that no nation would dare to provoke the United States to use it: "We will deter an enemy from making a nuclear attack only if our retaliatory power is so strong and so invulnerable that he knows he would be destroyed by our response."[39]

The United States Army Corps of Engineers' official construction history of the Abilene-area Atlas missile sites includes an April 20, 1961 editorial titled "A Bow to Dyess Missile Project" that began forebodingly:

> *This is not a game of tiddlywinks, the Cold War which pits democracy against communism. It should be soaking in on us that there is a grim issue of survival which overshadows.*
>
> *We face an enemy who is determined, ruthless and possessed of scientific skill and the new tools of warfare its science and monolithic government can produce.*

In a triumphal tone, however, the writer transitions to a discussion of the national Atlas missile program and the local efforts to build the twelve launch sites near Dyess Air Force Base:

We have great skill and knowhow. We put them to work with varying degrees of determination.

The U.S. is building, at various places about the nation, installations in which to place ballistic missiles.

Once in place, the missiles will be a powerful new deterrent. With them aimed at its heart, the Kremlin would think long and hard before committing suicide....

We cannot speak too highly, the nation cannot speak too highly of these men who have kept the local work churning....

According to the latest report we have, 978 persons are employed on the local missile projects. Of these, 469 have local (Abilene or other area towns) permanent addresses. They are homefolk. In all, 946 with permanent addresses have been employed on the jobs at one time or another.

The Dyess missile projects have meant much to local communities. But their importance is more than local.

The Air Force, in carrying out its missile assignment, is rushing to get the Atlas, the Titan, the Minuteman of the not too-distant future in place to protect this nation.

The AF is performing mightily in the face of the complexities of a new science—and in the face of some manmade complexities.

The contractors, the workers, the Air Force, all those involved in bringing the Dyess projects smoothly into being deserve the nation's deepest bow of gratitude. This is a most serious business and these people seem to realize it.[40]

Three weeks later, Manuel L. Arispe became the second Abilene-area missile site fatality. On May 9, 1961, at 10:25 a.m., Arispe, employed by H.B. Zachry Company, fell 96 feet from the Albany silo's fifth level to the bottom. While passing an iron piece to a coworker as he placed air conditioning ducts in the silo, he fell backward through the elevator shaft and struck a beam. An Abilene doctor was called to the site, where he pronounced Arispe dead an hour later. A Winters native, Arispe had been on the job about four months.[41]

The third missile-site fatality—and second at Oplin—happened just one week later. On May 16, Bobby Wayne Ragsdale, an electrician for H.B. Zachry Company and Brown and Root Inc., was electrocuted. At eight

This page: Construction of Dyess Air Force Base–area Atlas F missile launch site in the early 1960s. *Defense Visual Information Distribution Service.*

Above and opposite: Construction of Dyess Air Force Base–area Atlas F missile launch site in the early 1960s. *Defense Visual Information Distribution Service.*

thirty in the evening, Ragsdale touched a 480-volt switch gear while working on the silo's second floor, after which he was taken to Hendrick Memorial Hospital in Abilene, where he was pronounced dead. This was the third Abilene-area site death in just over six weeks; shortly before these deaths, the H.B. Zachry Company and Brown and Root Inc. had earned the top safety marks among the nation's Atlas missile site construction projects for their missile site work.[42]

The *Abilene Reporter-News* announced to its readers in the June 21, 1961 edition that contractor H.B. Zachry transferred ownership of the Oplin site to United States Air Force lieutenant colonel A.M. Antonelli of the Corps of Engineers Ballistic Missile Construction Office. Site completion was significant because in addition to being the first area site to finish the first construction phase, it was the nation's first Atlas site to be finished by the original completion date specified in its contract. The event was marked by a ribbon-cutting at the site's launch control center entrance, after which Antonelli turned over the keys to Colonel Hugh B. Manson, Dyess AFB

commander of the Site Activation Task Force located there. Manson then led military and civilian event attendees on a tour of both the LCC and missile silo. According to the story, "Visitors to the site trooped down a flight of concrete steps and through double 'blast doors' designed to protect those inside from even a nuclear blast. One visitor was heard to comment that it looked like a good storm cellar." The Corps of Engineers also presented a certificate to Zachry with this inscription: "Presented to H.B. Zachry-Brown and Root on the occasion of the turnover of the Oplin Launch Complex of the Dyess Atlas Missile Site on the original contract date. This unique achievement, which defied a compressed time schedule, required the utmost of construction skill and is indicative of a high order of competence, initiative and patriotism." The story also relayed that once the site reached operational readiness, it would be turned over General Dynamics Astronautics, the Atlas missile manufacturer.[43]

A July 10, 1961 editorial in the Abilene newspaper announced that the next phase of site construction had begun, and it would bring hundreds of jobs to the area. "Brown and Root Construction Co. of Houston was given a sub-contract by General Dynamics-Astronautics for installation, maintenance modification and repair of the ground support and operations equipment at the 12 missile silos," the editorial relayed. Up to eight hundred people would be hired, including many locals, for the fourteen-month construction time frame for the second construction phase. The editorial went on to speculate that "even with an awareness that we are living in a missile age, it is doubtful that many Abilene and area residents have really felt the drama of the history that is unfolding here in our back yard." The editorialist believed that although Abilene was accustomed to a military presence and had been since before World War II, "here we see being built the facilities that mark the most drastic change in weaponry in the world's history of warfare. Upon these bases, if they are ever needed in actual war, will hinge the survival not only of our nation, but the whole civilization of free mankind."[44]

The fourth Dyess-area fatality occurred at the Anson site. At nine in the morning on July 26, 1961, Robert A. Harralson, a pipefitter, fell from a scaffold at level 7 while unloading steel and fell more than 60 feet to the silo floor. No one witnessed the accident, but Harralson's coworkers speculated that he either became dizzy or was struck by a falling object, lost his balance and fell. He was working as a pipefitter for Paul Hardeman Company, which was hired as a subcontractor by Zachry-Brown, to install the Atlas missile propellant loading system at each site.[45]

The 577th Strategic Missile Squadron at Altus Air Force Base in southwest Oklahoma also operated twelve Atlas F ICBMs, one of which was housed in a launch complex just south of the Red River, about ten miles north of Vernon near Fargo in northern Wilbarger County. In addition to the four Dyess-area fatalities, one man died while working at the Fargo Atlas missile site. Construction worker Keith Arnold was preparing for concrete to be poured on the launch control center at the Fargo site on the morning of March 24, 1961, when he fell approximately thirty feet to his death. Arnold's pregnant wife, unaware of her husband's accident, was admitted about an hour after his death to the hospital in Vernon to give birth.[46]

Because of the Berlin crisis following the June 1961 meeting between President Kennedy and Soviet leader Nikita Khrushchev at Vienna, Austria, when Khrushchev issued a six-month deadline for Americans to leave West Berlin or face a likely war, the same edition of the Abilene newspaper that announced the fourth Dyess-area site fatality also carried multiple Associated Press stories about the Kennedy administration's attempt to immediately increase defense spending. One story referenced the appearance by Secretary of Defense Robert McNamara that day before the Senate Appropriations Committee to explain the need to strengthen American forces in Europe in response to possible Soviet action against Berlin. McNamara told the

Senate committee that President Kennedy's request of an additional $3.5 billion would bolster the American position in Berlin and better enable the United States to respond to "Communist threats and pressure all around the globe," including Southeast Asia. Another AP story about the Kennedy request for immediate increased defense spending referenced the president's announcement the previous evening that the nation would repel with force any attempt by the Soviet Union to drive the Americans out of West Berlin, a position that the United States had maintained since the end of World War II in 1945. Eager to stop the mass exodus each year of hundreds of thousands of East Germans fleeing Communism through Berlin, Khrushchev stopped access from East Berlin into West Berlin on August 13, 1961 by erecting the Berlin Wall—first a temporary barbed wire fence, followed eventually by the permanent stone wall that would divide the city for another twenty-eight years.[47] Shortly afterward, President Kennedy sent Vice President Johnson to Berlin to calm fears that the United States would abandon the city. Johnson addressed three hundred thousand West Berliners and reassured them that the United States was committed to defending them and their beleaguered city with "our lives, our fortunes, and our sacred honor."[48]

The United States Air Force formally accepted the twelfth and final Dyess-area Atlas F missile site on November 3, 1961. Air Force personnel and the prime contractor were recognized with awards for excellence during ceremonies that day. The official Corps of Engineers construction history includes a ribbon-cutting ceremony photograph that shows Major General Thomas P. Gerrity; Colonel Hugh B. Manson of Dyess Air Force Base; Winters, Texas, mayor Harvey Jones; H.B. Zachry, president of H.B. Zachry Company; local businessman W.P. Wright; Lieutenant Colonel Albert M. Antonelli; Major General Alvin C. Welling; Colonel Thomas B. Hayes; and H.B. Zachry Company/Brown and Root Inc. project manager D.V. Moore.[49]

The first Atlas F missile designated for one of the Abilene-area launch sites was flown by a C-133B transport from San Diego, California, to Dyess AFB and unloaded the morning of December 6, 1961. That afternoon, the missile was moved to the base's missile assembly building to be evaluated by both General Dynamics Astronautics and the Air Force Site Activation Task Force. Each air force base that operated Atlas missiles utilized a missile assembly building, or MAB, that housed a spare ICBM and provided space for each operational missile to undergo periodic maintenance after being removed from operational status. Every Atlas missile included three hundred thousand parts. At the same time that the missile's arrival made news, the

This page: Atlas F missile en route to its Dyess Air Force Base–area launch site, circa 1962. *Defense Visual Information Distribution Service.*

Atlas F missile on display in Abilene, circa 1962. *Defense Visual Information Distribution Service.*

Associated Press reported that the Soviet Union's government announced an unprecedently high budget for 1962 driven by a dramatic increase in defense spending, which began the previous July in response to the massive increase in American defense spending in response to the Berlin crisis. The Soviet government announced a budgetary increase of 13.4 billion rubles, or $14.74 billion, from 1961.[50]

In May 1962, General Dynamics Astronautics employees T.J. Colston and W.B. Cozart saved taxpayers $1 million by saving one of the Abilene-area Atlas missiles from deflating. Though made of steel, each missile's

This page and opposite: Dyess Air Force Base–area Atlas F missile raised on its elevator in launch position, circa 1962. *Defense Visual Information Distribution Service.*

outer skin was extremely thin—narrower than a dime—and the missile, compared by some to a giant balloon, required constant air pressure to remain inflated. One evening, an air pressure hose attached to an Atlas missile broke, and air began escaping from the ICBM. Colston and Cozart quickly thrust their hands across the missile fitting to prevent further air escape until the hose could be reattached. Both suffered cuts in the process and were afterward awarded commendation letters and small models of the $1 million missile that they saved from GDA operations manager R.C. Harbert and commander of Dyess AFB Site Activation Task Force Colonel Hugh B. Manson.[51]

In mid-October 1962, the nation—and the world—entered into the most dangerous two weeks of the Cold War. The Kennedy administration learned that the Soviet Union was building sites in Cuba capable of launching nuclear missiles against the United States, and the Cuban Missile Crisis began. Because of the crisis, all twelve missiles assigned to the 578th Strategic Missile Squadron at Dyess Air Force Base were placed on alert.[52] President Kennedy made a televised address the evening of October 22 and informed the nation about the Soviet imposition of missile bases in Cuba and that he was ordering a naval blockade—called a quarantine—there to prevent further offensive Soviet weapons from reaching the island. Under the banner heading "JFK Orders Cuban Blockade," the October 23, 1962 edition of the *Abilene Reporter-News* announced measures being taken by the United States government in response to the unfolding Cuban crisis. The day after President Kennedy addressed the nation, the Abilene newspaper carried Associated Press stories titled "U.S. Prepared to Sink Ships" and "Reds Increase Nuclear Threat," regarding the Soviet missiles in Cuba and American plans to blockade Cuba's coast. A local story in that edition said that military officials in Abilene refused to comment when asked Monday night after President Kennedy's address if local units were placed on alert.[53]

President Kennedy formed the Executive Committee of the National Security Council, or EXCOMM, to meet secretly before the president's television address and devise a strategy to eliminate the Soviet missile threat in Cuba. Vice President Johnson was a committee member, though he played only a minor role, rarely speaking during EXCOMM meetings.[54] Fortunately, the Cuban crisis ended peacefully, and none of Texas's intercontinental ballistic missiles were fired toward a Communist enemy, nor would they ever be.

An Atlas missile display was scheduled for the September 1963 West Texas Fair in Abilene. The local newspaper described the attraction as "a full-scale mock-up of the Atlas missile, the trademark of America's space

President Kennedy meets with Executive Committee of the National Security Council (EXCOMM) members, including Vice President Lyndon Johnson, concerning the Cuban Missile Crisis, October 29, 1962. *John F. Kennedy Presidential Library and Museum.*

exploration program." With identical dimensions to the Atlas missiles surrounding Abilene, the fair replica also included a display area at its base through which fairgoers could walk. The story reminded readers that "the mighty Atlas stands 24-hour guard duty daily in 12 sites ringing Abilene. Described as 'the work horse of the space age,' the intercontinental ballistic missile has been used in the man-in-space program and is slated for more advanced missions."[55]

When the axle bearings on one of the ground-level silo doors at the Corinth West missile site malfunctioned, the cost estimate to repair the door was $7,000. Base engineer Charles Ferguson decided that the door could be repaired faster and less expensively by local personnel, so nine members of the Civil Engineering Squadron were chosen as the door repair team, one of whom was Robert Breeding. Breeding acquired the tools for the job, including a forty-ton crane, which was loaned by General Dynamics Astronautics. Louis Jackson of the Dyess sheet metal shop created special tools for the repair. Not only had this crew not performed this operation before, but its members had never even seen it done. The faulty silo door was opened, and Airman Second Class Ross McIntire welded braces to keep the door in place during the repair. Other crew members were Kenneth Garner; Staff Sergeant Julian Robak; Airmen John Koss, Guy Sutherland and James Smith; and Technical Sergeant Louis Brooks. The silo doors were so heavy

Dyess Air Force Base–area Atlas F missile protruding through the open silo doors, circa 1962. *Defense Visual Information Distribution Service.*

that only one end of the faulty door could be hoisted by the crane at a time. The job began at eight in the morning, and after fifteen hours of painstaking work, ended successfully at eleven o'clock, at a cost of only $1,000.[56]

Between June 1, 1963, and March 9, 1964, three Atlas F sites attached to Walker Air Force Base in New Mexico were destroyed during propellant loading exercises. On May 14, 1964, an Atlas F site attached to Altus Air Force Base in Oklahoma was also destroyed by an explosion during a propellant loading exercise. Two days after the Oklahoma explosion, Secretary of Defense Robert McNamara announced that the Atlas E series would be phased out by the end of fiscal year 1965. Because they were considered obsolete, in November 1964, Secretary McNamara announced that all first-generation American ICBMs—including the Atlas F—would be retired the following year.[57]

The Abilene newspaper announced that the Atlas missiles were leaving the Abilene area in its November 19, 1964 edition. It carried an Associated Press story that, using information provided by Congressman Omar Burleson, informed readers that the twelve area missile launch sites would be closed by March 31, 1965. Secretary McNamara announced that all of the nation's Atlas E, Atlas F and Titan I ICBM bases would close early the

Lawn Atlas F missile site Launch Control Center entrance/exit, December 3, 2020. *Defense Visual Information Distribution Service.*

Lawn Atlas F missile site staircase leading to the Launch Control Center and missile silo, December 3, 2020. *Defense Visual Information Distribution Service.*

Front page of the November 19, 1964 *Abilene Reporter-News. newspaperarchive.com.*

next year. The newer Titan II and Minuteman ICBMs were replacing the older, obsolescent missiles as the United States government sought ways to both modernize its nuclear deterrent and save money.[58]

Although the Dyess-area Atlas missile sites were closing and most of the 950 men of the 578th Strategic Missile Squadron (SMS) were being relocated to other Air Force bases, the December 4, 1964 edition of the Abilene newspaper reported that some would remain at Dyess AFB to fill openings. The loss of $2.58 million of the 578th SMS's $5.15 million yearly payroll would, however, be offset in part by the $2.4 million payroll of a refueling unit that was scheduled to arrive from El Paso. These figures were updated by the December 30, 1964 edition of the *Abilene Reporter-News*, which carried a story listing the 1965 Dyess total payroll declining from $25.4 million to $24.3 million, a loss of $1.1 million, and 380 men employed there. These figures were provided during remarks made to the Abilene Chamber of Commerce the same day by Colonel Harold A. Radetsky, commander of the Ninety-Sixth Strategic Aerospace Wing at Dyess Air Force Base, which oversaw the twelve area Atlas missile sites. The story mentioned a KC-135 jet tanker squadron that was moving to Dyess AFB and bringing 500 men with it, and the 95 men who were scheduled to return from Eglin Air Force Base in Florida.[59]

The first Dyess AFB Atlas F was taken off alert status on December 1, 1964. Strategic Air Command headquarters inactivated the 578th Strategic

Missile Squadron at Dyess AFB and the 577th Strategic Missile Squadron at Altus Air Force Base, which operated the Fargo Atlas F launch site in Wilbarger County, on March 25, 1965.[60]

The first Atlas F ICBM that arrived in Abilene in December 1961 left for California on the morning of January 11, 1965. Three years and one month after becoming the first missile to arrive at Dyess AFB, the missile known as the Spirit of Oplin left for Norton Air Force Base near San Bernardino, California, where all the other Dyess-area missiles would also be sent. Less than one month later, the final Atlas missile was shipped from the Baird site to Norton AFB on February 10. Air Force personnel who worked the last missile shift included Captain Wesley M. Warr, Captain George F. Wortell, First Lieutenant Edward L. Barre, Technical Sergeant Seth D. Ragen, Airman Second Class James W. Cothran, Stanley G. Wilson and Staff Sergeant Fidelo A. Atencio. The 578th Strategic Missile Squadron operated the Dyess-area Atlas missiles for nearly three years and enjoyed the distinction of doing so without any ICBM accidents.[61]

According to Lonnquest and Winkler, all thirteen Texas Atlas F missile launch complexes—the twelve Dyess-area sites and the Fargo site—were sold to private owners. They described each of the thirteen Texas Atlas missile sites with these words in 1996: "Current: Private ownership, materials salvaged before sold but structure remains intact."[62]

NIKE

The Soviet acquisition of atomic weapons in 1949 forced the United States to prepare to defend against a Soviet atomic attack by airplane. A reevaluation of American foreign and defense policy occasioned by multiple events, including the American loss of its atomic monopoly to the Soviets, resulted in the 1950 document known as NSC 68. The paper stated that by 1954, the Soviet Union would have a large stockpile of atomic bombs and the ability to deliver them inside the United States, requiring dramatic increases in defense spending. To strengthen its defensive capabilities against such a Soviet long-range bomber attack, the United States sped up its work on the Nike surface-to-air missile. The U.S. Army began developing the Nike Ajax antiaircraft missile in 1945, with deployment of the first Nike battery in 1954. The liquid-fueled Ajax was thirty-four feet long, had a thirty-mile range, could operate at an altitude of 70,000 feet and carried a conventional bomb. In 1958, two hundred Nike batteries were scattered across the nation.

Dyess Air Force Base–area Nike Hercules missile, circa 1960. *Hardin-Simmons University Library.*

The same year, the Army deployed the newer Nike Hercules as it began phasing out the Ajax. The solid-fueled Hercules was forty-one feet long, had a seventy-five-mile range and was operational at an altitude of up to 150,000 feet. The first among antiaircraft missiles to carry a nuclear warhead, the Nike Hercules was deployed at 137 locations.[63]

Whereas America's ICBMs were housed in rural locations, the Nike launch sites were near the nation's large cities and surrounding metropolitan areas. The sites, built beginning in the late 1950s, stood only one story, were made of cinderblocks and reportedly resembled the many school buildings built to accommodate baby boom children who filled schools during the decade. By 1958, just five years after the army received permission to develop a second-generation surface-to-air missile, the Nike Hercules was ready for deployment near New York, Chicago and Philadelphia. In the late 1950s and early '60s, the Hercules was positioned close to cities in the middle of the country as well as near several Strategic Air Command bases.[64]

Bergstrom Air Force Base housed army personnel who defended the Strategic Air Command base as well as the Austin area from two Nike Hercules sites. One was designated BG-40 and was located southeast of Elroy, and the other was designated BG-80 and was located west/northwest of Austin. Headquarters for these Nike Hercules batteries were at Bergstrom AFB, and they were operational from November 1960 to June 1966.[65]

The January 9, 1959 edition of the *Taylor Daily Press* announced that Taylor "would be near the center of a 20,000 square-mile area to be defended by two U.S. Army Nike Hercules missile battery sites near Austin." The story described one site as being five miles west of Austin on Bee Cave Road, with the other Bergstrom Defense Area site being "approximately 13 miles southeast of Austin in Bastrop County near the Travis County line." The story projected costs for each battery, which could defend a 20,000-square-mile area in and around Austin, to be more than $1 million. Each battery was going to be built on two plots of land, each no more than a mile and a half apart. "One of the tracts, known as the integrated fire control (IFC) area, will contain the radars and electronic computers of the guidance system," the story said. "The other tract, the launcher area, will contain the missile handling and storage facilities, including the missile launchers." Each site would also include barracks, administration buildings and mess halls, and housing would be required for married personnel, some of whom were required to live close enough to their work to arrive within five minutes. According to the story, about one hundred enlisted men and eight officers would operate each site, and this would require a $25,000 monthly payroll.[66]

Four Nike Hercules batteries defended the Dallas–Forth Worth area. Site DF-01, operated from September 1960 until October 1968, was located north of Denton; site DF-20, operated from August 1960 until February 1964, was northeast of Terrell; site DF-50, operated from August 1960 until October

1968, was southeast of Alvarado; site DF-70, operated from September 1960 until October 1968, was located at Fort Wolters. Headquarters for all four sites were located at Duncanville Air Force Station. The Army Corps of Engineers Fort Worth District was responsible for building these facilities, each of which sat on thirty acres. Cost for land acquisition and site construction, which began in 1958, was $1.5 million per site. These sites were operated by both Regular Army and National Guard personnel.[67]

The *Abilene Reporter-News* announced in its August 6, 1959 edition that Nike Hercules site construction would soon begin. The contract for building the two Abilene-area Nike Hercules sites was won by Browning Construction Company, which submitted a bid of $1,674,830. According to Colonel Walter J. Wells of the Corps of Engineers, construction was to begin within the next few weeks, and Browning Construction would be obligated to complete all work within 240 days. Construction cost for the site southwest of Abilene was projected to be $884,411, and the site northeast of Abilene would cost $790,419.[68]

On May 1, 1960, American pilot Francis Gary Powers was shot down while flying a reconnaissance mission over the Soviet Union for the Central Intelligence Agency to determine the Soviets' nuclear weapons capability. Two weeks later, the Abilene newspaper reported that the Nike Hercules site near Lake Fort Phantom was being used by military personnel the previous day, and meals were being served in the base mess hall. The story included a photo by Don Hutcheson showing four men in military uniforms unloading a truck, with this caption: "MOVING IN—Four members of the 5th Missile Battalion, 517th Artillery, move into new quarters at the Nike Hercules missile firing site north of Abilene on the west side of Lake Fort Phantom. Sgt. 1.C. Russel Lovenz (left) checks off the equipment being unloaded by (left to right) Sp. 4.C. Donald R Harms, Sp. 4.C. Richard Baker and Sgt. Charles Inman." The story said that the other Abilene-area Nike Hercules site near View would be completed about a month later.[69]

One week later, the Abilene public was made aware that high-ranking army officials, led by Major General Phillip H. Draper Jr., deputy commander of the U.S. Army Air Defense Command, would be in town to view tests at the Nike Hercules site north of Abilene. This was the first aboveground launch site constructed for the Nike Hercules, which became the model for similar sites around the nation. The battalion's first Nike missile had recently arrived in Abilene, which would allow it to conduct the first firing simulation under Chief Warrant Officer Woodrow W. Zellers. The local newspaper provided this site description: "The local sites are at ground level, with earth

Aerial view of control site for Nike Hercules Battery DY-10 north of Abilene, circa 1960. *Hardin-Simmons University Library.*

bunkers around each pair of missiles. An igloo-like balloon canopy, which can be collapsed instantly, is used to protect them against weather."[70]

The same page of the same edition carried a story explaining to Abilene residents the differences between the Nike Hercules missile and the Atlas F missile. The Atlas was much larger—its dimensions were provided—and it was described as capable of delivering a nuclear bomb to its target inside the Soviet Union within thirty minutes of launch from Abilene. The Atlas missile was a retaliatory air force weapon that was overseen by Dyess Air Force Base personnel. The Nike Hercules, on the other hand, was an army antiaircraft weapon that would only be used to defend Dyess AFB and the West Texas Defense Area by shooting down enemy aircraft during an attack. The story ended by affirming that the Atlas and Nike Hercules missiles near Abilene would only be launched in response to an attack.[71]

Two months later, the public was invited by battalion commander Colonel Joseph P. Guinn to an August open house at the two Abilene-area Nike Hercules missile sites. The newspaper story about the sites

Four Dyess Air Force Base–area Nike Hercules missiles, circa 1960. *Hardin-Simmons University Library.*

characterized the missiles housed there as "surface-to-air missile[s] with a 'released' range of 75 miles." A photo of the Lake Phantom Nike site accompanied the story, and the caption beneath pointed out the living and dining quarters and administrative offices and referenced battalion executive officer Major Charles W. Nolen, who told military editor H.V. O'Brien that no Nike Hercules missile had unintentionally detonated at any Texas site. He followed that up by reassuring the Abilene public that no harm would befall anyone near the site when nuclear warheads were mounted on those missiles. The story also included a map showing the two protection areas provided by the two batteries near Abilene, as well as Nike Hercules sites near Dallas-Fort Worth.[72]

One week later, H.V. O'Brien wrote that the following day, San Antonio general contractor R.J. Browning would transfer control of the View Nike site, designated "Battery B site of the 5th Missile Battalion, 517th Artillery," to the army. O'Brien described the site's location as "six miles south of View on the San Angelo highway." O'Brien also reported that on Friday,

A map showing locations defended by Nike Hercules missile batteries in the Abilene and Dallas–Fort Worth areas. *Hardin-Simmons University Library.*

a Fort Hood technical maintenance team would inspect the site "for Capt. Henry G. Trinkner, commander of the 3rd Surface-to-Air Missile Support detachment" and that "Trinkner and his staff of five military personnel and 43 civilians provide all supplies and maintenance support for Abilene's Nike-Hercules Missile Battalion." The Battery B commander, Captain Elgin L. Eskridge, told O'Brien that the 110-man unit would move into the site's buildings over the next few days. O'Brien also reported that battalion headquarters and a "missile support building" were being built at Dyess AFB. Construction would also take place at Sweetwater Air Force Station for personnel and equipment "which will tie the Abilene Nike-Hercules Defense to the North American Defense Command," or NORAD. O'Brien explained that NORAD answered to the United States Joint Chiefs of Staff as well as Canada's government in defending the entire North American continent against attack by air. Abilene's Davis Brothers Construction Company was listed as contractor for the headquarters buildings, and the motor pool contractor was Cooke and Sons, also of Abilene. The missile shop building contract was awarded to San Antonio's Harwell and Harwell Construction Company.[73]

An early January 1966 story in the *Abilene Reporter-News* by military editor Bob Bruce looked back at the consequential year for Dyess Air Force Base that had just passed. Bruce reminded his readers that on December 6, the Department of Defense announced $419 million in military spending reductions that would eliminate Abilene's Nike Hercules missiles in 1966 and Dyess's B-52 bombers by 1971. He also reflected on the previous year's ending of Dyess's ICBM program and the 578th Strategic Missile Squadron's operations there in March, also guided by Defense Department spending cuts. The story included four photographs with the caption, "Decade's Arsenal: The bombers and missiles which have typified the defense posture at Dyess AFB during the past 10 years are shown here: B-52 Stratofortress and B-47 Stratojet, Atlas ICBM and Nike-Hercules anti-aircraft missile. The B-47 and Atlas already are gone, the Nike is to depart by mid-1966, and the B-52 is due to be phased out by 1971. The year 1965 marked the 10th year of operations at Dyess."[74]

In the spring of 1962, Captain Joseph Mella set out to grant the wish of Abilene's Nike Hercules commander, Lieutenant Colonel Joe Guinn, for a missile marker in front of headquarters. Without any extra actual missiles to use for a marker, Mella searched the Army's El Paso McGregor (test) Range for used missile parts. Except for two parts that had to be built by civilians Bill Dehnel and Wayne Owen, enough parts were shipped to Dyess to create a missile marker. To erect the marker and make it impervious to West Texas winds, concrete was poured over steel bars inside the marker's bottom four feet, anchoring the mock missile in the ground. The job required thirty-two hours over two days. When the 1966 inactivation of the Dyess area's Nike Hercules missile program was announced in December 1965, the decision was made to transfer the marker to the Fourth Missile Battalion's Dallas–Fort Worth headquarters, and it was placed there on March 25, 1966. A brief announcement appeared beside this story that twenty-two-year-old Ranger High School graduate and army specialist Charles A. McCain was leaving for Vietnam, where he was joining the Seventy-First Artillery on a missile launch crew.[75]

The March 20, 1966 edition of the *Abilene Reporter-News* announced that the army's presence at Dyess Air Force Base would end on June 25 with the closure of the nearby army Nike Hercules missile bases, resulting from military spending cuts announced by Secretary of Defense Robert McNamara. The air force was scheduled to assume control of the buildings formerly occupied

Dyess Air Force Base–area Nike Hercules missile, circa 1960. *Hardin-Simmons University Library.*

by the Fifth Missile Battalion. Eight Strategic Air Command (SAC) bases were losing their Nike missile programs, including Austin's Bergstrom Air Force Base. According to the article, "Civilian caretakers, employed by the Army Engineers at Fort Hood, Tex., [were] in charge of the Phantom and Barkely firing sites," until the General Services Administration was prepared to assume control of the property "for disposal." Some of the officers and enlisted men at the eight SAC bases that were closing would be transferred to Vietnam, including about twenty from Dyess. Some were bound for duty with other missile units, while others were headed to the army's missile school at Fort Bliss in El Paso.[76]

A United Press International story appearing in the August 17, 1968 edition of the *San Antonio Light* announced that another group of twenty-three Nike Hercules missile sites around the nation was closing. Part of an effort to reduce military spending by $3 billion, the closures were projected to save $18.8 million during the fiscal year ending June 30 and $54 million each subsequent fiscal year. Defense Department officials said this would not adversely affect the nation's ability to defend against manned bomber attack, and the story went on to reference the diminished Soviet long-range bomber threat and increased threat from that nation's intercontinental ballistic missiles. Among the Nike Hercules sites closing were those at Denton, Alvarado, Camp Wolters and Terrell, and "Headquarters installations" closing included two in Duncanville.[77]

In 1996, according to Lonnquest and Winkler, the Alvarado site was privately owned; the Denton site was owned by the Denton Board of Education; the Texas Army National Guard owned the Fort Wolters site and used it for training, as well as small arms storage, firing and maneuvering; the Terrell site was owned by the Terrell School District and was used by the Future Farmers of America (FFA) program and for school bus storage and maintenance. Lonnquest and Winkler also listed the BG-80 Austin site as belonging to the Texas Army National Guard 111th Support Group, and they listed the BG-40 Austin site as being privately owned.[78]

As the United States Air Force characterized it, the advent of the ICBM force in 1960 ushered in an "uneasy half-peace" between the United States and the Soviet Union. Though conflicts arose, nuclear war did not. According to Jacob Neufeld in *The Development of Ballistic Missiles in the United States Air Force 1945–1960*, both sides enhanced their stockpiles of ICBMs "over the years to ensure their ability to inflict 'unacceptable damage' upon the enemy under any conditions." Possession of possibly civilization-altering weapons gave both sides pause. As Neufeld put it, ICBMs were "a paradox—thousands of them waiting to unleash total destruction, but the very fact of their presence ensuring their non-use."[79]

The Kennedy administration operated with the hope that the Soviet Union would not initiate a nuclear war knowing that both countries would be destroyed. This was the essence of the doctrine of mutual assured destruction, or MAD.[80] Signaling his agreement with this philosophy, during the October 1962 Cuban Missile Crisis, Soviet leader Nikita Khrushchev pleaded with President Kennedy by letter to join him in taking the necessary steps to avoid "the catastrophe of thermonuclear war" between the two countries, because "only lunatics or suicides, who themselves want to perish and to destroy the whole world before they die," could allow such a war to happen.[81] During the crisis, one of Secretary of Defense Robert McNamara's aides explained that 841 American nuclear weapons would survive a Soviet first strike against the United States that did not include the Cuban missiles, and even a Soviet first strike that included the Cuban missiles would leave the United States with more than 480 nuclear weapons with which to retaliate—including most of the hardened underground missile sites—and inflict much greater damage on the Soviet Union than had been inflicted on the United States. In October 1962, the United States possessed 240 long-range missiles capable of reaching the Soviet Union—144 ICBMs and 96 missiles aboard Polaris submarines.[82] Nikita Khrushchev was keenly aware of the American nuclear arsenal's destructive capability, which moved him to implore President Kennedy to join him in avoiding nuclear war. That arsenal included 12 Atlas F ICBMs near Dyess Air Force Base and one at Fargo in northern Wilbarger County.

The Atlas F missile sites in Texas were operational for only a few years, and they were extremely costly—both in terms of money and the five lives lost—to build and operate. Millions were also spent building state Nike Hercules missile sites. As these missile sites were an integral part of a national security priority that spanned presidencies from Eisenhower in the 1950s to Lyndon Johnson in the late 1960s, little monetary expense was spared in program development and site construction. Businesses reaped the benefits of constructing those missile sites, and hundreds of Texans and others benefited from site-related job opportunities as Texans learned to live with nuclear weapons in their midst as part of daily life. The state benefited economically, but the nation benefited from Texas's missiles, because they defended Americans against possible attack and strengthened the American nuclear arsenal that deterred Soviet aggression and saved the nation from catastrophe.

CHAPTER 3

LONE STAR STATE CIVIL DEFENSE

As the Cold War moved into the nuclear age and tensions with the Soviet Union heightened, all Americans, including Texans, learned to live with the threat of nuclear war. To increase the likelihood of survival if nuclear war came, national, state and local civil defense organizations took steps to protect the public. Civil defense preparedness became part of everyday life across the nation and across the state as Texas communities prepared to survive a nuclear attack.

In light of the Soviet Union's breaking the American atomic monopoly and acquiring an atomic bomb in 1949, Congress passed, and President Truman signed into law, the Federal Civil Defense Act of 1950, creating the Federal Civil Defense Administration (FCDA). According to B. Wayne Blanchard in *American Civil Defense 1945–1984: The Evolution of Programs and Policies*, to protect Americans against a Soviet attack, the FCDA envisioned "a three-stage shelter program which would (1) locate existing shelter, (2) upgrade potential shelter, and (3) construct new shelter in deficit areas in the Nation's 'critical target cities' as designated by the FCDA and the Department of Defense."[83]

The first Office of Civil Defense Planning director was Russell J. Hopley. Hopley, formerly president of Northwestern Bell Telephone of Omaha, Nebraska, was appointed in 1948, and within months he published the manual *Civil Defense for National Security* to educate the nation's citizens about steps they could take to protect themselves in an atomic war. Hopley's manual emphasized evacuating large cities prior to an atomic attack.

This "crisis relocation" philosophy was replaced with a shelter-centric approach, and the federal government encouraged Americans to build their own home fallout shelters. CBS television aired a program called *Retrospect*, and an episode in the early 1950s featured the Brown family of Topeka, Kansas. The family, two parents and their eight children, was asked about the week they spent in their recently built home fallout shelter. The *Encyclopedia of the Great Plains* characterized such civil defense efforts as "little more than a psychological salve for the American populace" because President Eisenhower's administration realized by the middle of the 1950s "that nuclear war meant national suicide. Nevertheless, the administration continued to promote the myth of personal responsibility for civil defense in order to avoid demoralizing the American public."[84]

President Eisenhower believed that while the federal government could provide guidance for civil defense, the bulk of those responsibilities lay with state and local governments. However, after learning of the extremely dangerous "blast and thermal effects" of the American hydrogen bomb detonation in 1952, the Soviet Union's hydrogen bomb detonation in 1953 and "the March 1954 BRAVO hydrogen bomb explosion," American policymakers became concerned about "the lethal hazard of long-range radioactive fallout." Many in the American government recognized the danger posed by fallout's spread over thousands of miles after a nuclear explosion, which moved Chet Holified, chair of the House Military Operations Subcommittee, to scrutinize the Eisenhower administration's civil defense policy. Representative Holified sponsored H.R. 2125, a bill to elevate civil defense to the cabinet level, emphasizing the primacy of the federal government's civil defense role and establishing a national fallout shelter program. The FCDA followed suit and proposed a $32 billion national shelter program.[85]

President Eisenhower assigned a committee to study the FCDA shelter plan in April 1957. The Security Resources Panel of the Science Advisory Committee was chaired by H. Rowan Gaither and was known popularly as the Gaither Committee. The committee made several recommendations to President Eisenhower and the National Security Council, including improving the Strategic Air Command forces, hastening development of intercontinental and intermediate-range ballistic missiles, fortifying intercontinental ballistic missile (ICBM) locations, enlarging American forces and diminishing the vulnerability of American cities. The committee suggested a "passive defense" strategy featuring a $25 billion national program for nuclear fallout shelters to save lives in the event of a nuclear war. Pressure on Eisenhower mounted, caused by two momentous events that year. In August, the Soviet Union launched the first ICBM. Then, in October, the Soviets launched the first artificial satellite, Sputnik, into orbit. Eisenhower responded by merging the FCDA and the Office of Defense Mobilization to create the Office of Civil Defense Mobilization. The administration called on state and local governments to coordinate in creating a national shelter system while merely receiving "advice and guidance" from the federal government.[86]

Eisenhower was loathe to spend the huge sums of money necessary for a nationwide shelter program, even as policymakers in Washington considered the value of "passive defense" versus "active defense." Delivered to President Eisenhower in November 1957, the Gaither Committee's report, *Deterrence and Survival in the Nuclear Age*, declared that by 1959 the United States would be extremely susceptible to a Soviet ICBM offensive, and it called for a $44 billion increase in defense spending over the next five years, which was greater than the 1958 defense budget. The new money would be split between bomber and missile acquisition, a national fallout shelter construction plan and other civil defense–related items.[87] As a United States senator, Lyndon B. Johnson spent the late 1950s investigating why the United States trailed the Soviet Union in space exploration. His efforts included hearings that resulted in legislation creating the National Aeronautics and Space Administration, NASA. Later, as vice president, Johnson chaired the National Aeronautics and Space Council, and he was integral in placing what became the Johnson Space Center in Houston.[88]

Though fiscally conservative and wanting to avoid increased spending on principle, Eisenhower also had another reason to shun calls for more weapons outlays: the U-2 spy plane had provided the president proof that the Soviet Union was not increasing its nuclear arsenal or airplane fleet in preparation for war. Because U-2 was a top-secret program used by the United States to spy on the Soviet Union, Eisenhower did not want to reveal this information or its source, and pressure on Eisenhower to catch up to the Soviet Union mounted. Yet Eisenhower also wanted to avoid falsely giving the impression to the Soviet government that the United States was preparing for war by building fallout shelters, which could increase the likelihood of war.[89]

The January 31, 1960 *Denton Record-Chronicle* dedicated an entire page to civil defense. One article looked ahead at Denton civil defense developments and their economic impact during the next decade, which included construction of an underground building operated by the Office of Civil and Defense Mobilization, part of the city's "federal complex." Other construction projects for federal facilities were projected to bring another 175 federal employees to town, which would boost the local economy. The same edition warned locals that rural dwellers faced danger from nuclear attack through radioactive fallout, and the nation's recovery depended heavily on farmers to provide the nation's population with food. With this in mind, the federal government was implementing a civil defense program for rural Americans, though specific program details were not provided. The newspaper also began educating readers about civil defense–related vocabulary with which they would need to be familiar in the 1960s, including "Continuity of Government," "Fallout," and "Public Information." Readers were reminded that the Office of Civil and Defense Mobilization had announced the previous summer that its Denton headquarters would be the nation's first underground regional control center, and the two-story facility would be designated as the third choice for the national control center if sites close to Washington, D.C., and in Battle Creek, Michigan, were leveled in an attack.[90]

North Runnels County began working toward creating a civil defense organization with a July 5, 1960 meeting at the Winters City Hall. W.R. Bodine with the Texas civil defense department was scheduled to meet with City Council members and civic groups. The Winters Lions Club formed a committee, led by Fred Young, to spearhead the meeting, and the group's plea to the public was that all Texans would be endangered by a Soviet nuclear attack, so even communities not directly impacted by such an attack would need to aid those that were.[91]

The *Daily Texan*, the University of Texas at Austin's student newspaper, warned readers in its October 14, 1960 edition that in the likely event of a nuclear war, Austin would probably be targeted. The publication quoted Colonel W.A. Kengla, the incoming Austin/Travis County civil defense director: "Austin has some acute problems in this respect. It is a logical target area with Bergstrom Air Force Base (a Strategic Air Command Base) and the state capitol in the same vicinity." Kengla also said that even if the capital city was spared but San Antonio's air force bases were attacked, Austin residents would still have to contend with radioactive fallout. The newspaper advised taking refuge in an underground shelter in the event of an attack and being prepared to stay there for two weeks while radiation in the atmosphere diminished. The story included a photo of two college students inside of a shelter with this caption: "Two UT girls, Linda Phillips and Linda Ivey, examine the civil defense shelter displayed at Zilker Park."[92]

The same edition of the student newspaper carried an Associated Press story about Soviet leader Nikita Khrushchev's appearance at the United Nations in New York City that closed his twenty-five-day visit to the United States. Though Khrushchev at times pounded his fist and even waived his shoe in anger at one point, he did claim that his country was prepared to consider nuclear disarmament. Beside this story was another Associated Press breakdown of the previous night's televised debate between presidential candidates John Kennedy and Richard Nixon. They sparred over defending the Quemoy and Matsu Islands off China's coast, the need to maintain an American presence in Berlin and the Communist government of Cuba.[93]

In April 1961, the University of Houston participated in a nationwide civil defense training called Operation Alert that included a mock nuclear attack. Information about the fictional attack was scheduled to be provided by North American Air Defense Headquarters (NORAD) and broadcast on Conelrad 640 and 1240 AM radio frequencies. The university's employees that composed the campus civil defense group were going to monitor Conelrad when the information was scheduled to be broadcast and forward it to the university community.[94]

President Kennedy assumed office appearing to view civil defense as a more urgent matter than President Eisenhower had. In a May 25, 1961 "Special Message to Congress on Urgent National Needs," President Kennedy articulated his desire to strengthen the nation's civil defense and enhance the federal government's role in providing it:

> *One major element of the national security program which this Nation has never squarely faced up to is civil defense. In the past decade we have considered a variety of programs, but we have never adopted a consistent policy....*
>
> *This administration has been looking very hard at exactly what civil defense can and cannot do. It cannot be obtained cheaply. It cannot give an assurance of blast protection that will be proof against surprise attack or guarantee against obsolescence or destruction. And it cannot deter a nuclear attack.*
>
> *We will deter an enemy from making a nuclear attack only if our retaliatory power is so strong and so invulnerable that he knows he would be destroyed by our response....*
>
> *But this deterrent concept assumes rational calculations by rational men. And the history of this planet is sufficient to remind us of the possibilities of an irrational attack, a miscalculation, or an accidental war which cannot*

be either foreseen or deterred. The nature of modern warfare heightens these possibilities. It is on this basis that civil defense can readily be justified—as insurance for the civilian population in the event of such a miscalculation. It is insurance which we could never forgive ourselves for foregoing in the event of catastrophe.[95]

To fund his new civil defense initiative, Kennedy followed this message by sending a July supplemental appropriations request of $207.6 million to Congress, which practically doubled the civil defense requests made during the Eisenhower presidency. Congress fully funded the request. The newly established Office of Civil Defense (OCD) utilized the funds and began a nationwide survey to identify existing buildings to be used as fallout shelters and to stock them with supplies.[96]

Fallout shelters were intended to protect citizens from radioactive nuclear fallout, which is what remains in the air after a nuclear explosion. In his article "In the Fallout Shelter: Civil Defense in Stillwater," civil defense historian James Gregory provided this explanation of fallout after such an explosion: "This dust is made radioactive by the nuclear explosion, and is blown miles downwind until falling back to earth. It then releases radioactivity until it decays." If the Soviet Union had attacked the United States with nuclear bombs, even Americans who avoided injury or death due to an explosion would have needed protection from drifting radioactive fallout until it decayed and no longer posed a threat. Shelters were intended to provide that protection.[97]

According to a 2006 report by the U.S. Department of Homeland Security, to qualify as a public shelter—which would be marked with what became the familiar fallout shelter sign that included three yellow triangles surrounded by a black circle—a space had to accommodate a minimum of fifty people, "include one cubic foot of storage space per person, and have a radiation protection factor of at least 100." The Defense Supply Agency within the Department of Defense provided supplies to local governments, which assumed responsibility for stocking the shelters in their area. The Department of Defense created the federal fallout shelter sign in December 1961, and one was placed on each shelter that met the federal government's criteria.[98]

The *Summer Texan* announced that Austin's civil defense sirens would be tested Friday, July 7, 1961, at ten in the morning. According to the UT student newspaper, the "test is part of Austin and Travis County's safeguard against what President Kennedy has called 'irrational attack'

Federal fallout shelter sign.
www.wikimedia.org.

or 'accidental war.'" The story also reminded readers that President Kennedy, "in his State of the Union speech, called for an increase in bomb shelter building and radio monitoring. He also made it evident that home-front defense is a partnership among all levels of government and its citizens."[99]

Stine Safety Shelters advertised in the September 3, 1961 edition of the *Amarillo Globe*. Offering "TORNADO AND RADIO ACTIVE [*sic*] FALLOUT PROTECTION," the company declared that its shelters came with the highest possible rating of "Almost Absolute Protection." Each underground shelter was built of reinforced concrete, though an explanation of what that meant was not included. Depending on the size of shelter purchased among the six options, as least four and as many as nine people could be accommodated. Each shelter also came with a "manually operated blower" and "hooded vents," and installation required three days.[100]

San Antonio Light columnist Morris Wilison, in the newspaper's October 9, 1961 edition, encouraged the city's families who were thinking of building home fallout shelters to visit the local civil defense office on South Alamo to gather information, including blueprints, for low-cost "shelters that could prove as priceless as life itself." He also relayed that informational brochures at the civil defense office explained that fallout would adversely impact more people than a nuclear blast itself; "radioactive fallout can spread death anywhere." He ended the brief piece by comparing a home fallout shelter to insurance, and he warned his readers to prepare for a nuclear attack before it happened.[101] Ironically, the same edition included a column by Joe Bishop, who asked Germans in their capital city if they believed that the issue of divided Berlin would be solved peacefully or result in a nuclear war. According to Bishop, Berliners and most Germans, signaling their adherence to the doctrine of mutual assured destruction, believed that the Soviets would never launch an unwinnable nuclear war against the United States. Knowing that neither side could prevail, nuclear war would not be initiated.[102]

Even the United States military attempted to provide fallout protection for its personnel. In late October 1961, Deputy Secretary of Defense Roswell Gilpatric instructed the secretaries of the various branches to undertake actions that would both protect service members and convey the seriousness with which the military took civil defense. Though money had not been allocated in the Defense Department budget for fallout shelters on military bases, some installations had begun designating existing space as fallout shelters. However, only the military members at the highest decision-making levels at locations such as the underground Strategic Air Command headquarters at Omaha, Nebraska, and the personnel who operated the belowground ICBM launch sites had access to large shelters equipped to withstand the highest levels of radiation. Gilpatric had a fallout shelter built at his home in Washington, D.C., and another built at his summer residence. Though his boss, Secretary of Defense Robert McNamara, had not built a shelter because he lived on rental property, McNamara's assistant in charge of civil defense, Adam Yarmolinsky, was having a shelter built at his home.[103]

According to *Amarillo Daily News* staff writer Jerry Langdon, in November 1961, Amarillo was believed to be one of three hundred United States locations that would be targeted by the Soviet Union during a nuclear attack. Amarillo Civil Defense Director Bob Roseberry believed that ten thousand Amarillo residents would have died and another thirty thousand would have been casualties the previous April had Operation Alert, the nationwide mock nuclear attack, been an actual attack with one-megaton nuclear bombs. The Soviet Union was, however, testing nuclear weapons with ten- to fifty-megaton bombs. Both state and national civil defense personnel had told Roseberry that Amarillo was ahead of most Texas cities in civil defense preparations, which included planning efforts by city utility providers to restore services after an attack. Roseberry was unsure of the number of Amarillo fallout shelters then. Though the Department of Defense would soon begin locating public spaces across the nation to serve as public shelters, Roseberry believed that home shelters were more practical for fallout protection. He had built his own shelter for $800.[104]

Portable civil defense hospitals were made available around the nation during the Kennedy presidency, one of which was on display in the Texas Panhandle in December 1961. Scheduled to be available for public view at the Tri-State Fairgrounds' Commercial Exhibits Building, the display was intended to allow both the general public and medical professionals to become familiar with the two-hundred-bed emergency hospital that could be operational just hours after a disaster. The emergency hospital would be disassembled and returned to West Texas State College in Canyon for storage, where it was overseen by Hugh T. Greiner, the college's superintendent of maintenance. If the hospital was needed following a disaster, members of the Teamsters Union Local No. 577 would drive the hospital to the disaster site. This disaster hospital was one of three in the Amarillo area.[105]

The United States Department of Defense published 25 million copies of a forty-eight-page booklet in late December 1961 for distribution at post offices and through both state and local civil defense groups in early January, explaining how Americans could survive a nuclear attack. The book's foreword included a grim admission that in such an attack, millions of Americans would die; however, millions of others could survive. The Defense Department declared that, because of the nation's nuclear deterrent, a nuclear attack was not likely. "However, should a nuclear attack ever occur, certain preparations could mean the difference between life and death for you." The booklet gave instructions for how to prepare to survive an attack that included a five-megaton nuclear bomb—equal to the explosive power of five million tons of TNT. The booklet's goal was to inform citizens how to survive a nuclear explosion's radioactive fallout. "No hope is held out for those who happen to be within the range of the blast, heat and initial radiation of the fusion bomb," the booklet stated; within ten miles of a nuclear explosion "would be scenes of havoc, devastation and death." The goal was for survivors beyond the lethal blast zone to seek shelter from fallout and remain there for up to two weeks, until leaving would be safe.[106]

The OCD created a handbook for citizens in January 1962 with instructions for building eight different kinds of home fallout shelters to be placed in basements or backyards to accommodate people who either lacked public shelter access or simply preferred shelter at home. The smallest shelter would accommodate three people and cost less than $75 to build, and the largest would accommodate ten people and cost approximately $550 to build. Each shelter was intended to be built as inexpensively as possible, which meant that most of the shelters required the homeowner to perform the construction. The eight different shelters were the "Basement Sand-Filled Lumber Lean-To Shelter," the "Basement Corrugated Asbestos-Cement Lean-To Shelter," the "Basement Concrete Block Shelter," the "Outside Semimounded Plywood Box Shelter," the "Belowground Corrugated Steel Culvert Shelter," the "Outside Semimounded Steel Igloo Shelter," the "Aboveground Earth-Covered Lumber A-Frame Shelter" and the "Belowground New Construction Clay Masonry Shelter." The last shelter was designed to be added to a new house under construction.[107]

The water drums provided by the federal government for local community shelters each held 17.5 gallons of water, which was intended to provide five people one quart of water a day for up to two weeks. Drums were made of

Federal civil defense water barrels and sanitation kits in storage. *Author.*

either fiberboard or, later, steel, and according to the Civil Defense Museum, each included two "plastic liners inside and stood about 22 inches tall and was about 16 inches in diameter." One liner held water, and the other liner was an extra to be used if needed. When filled with water, the polyethylene liners were either sealed with heat or tied. In normal conditions, the metal drums and polyethylene liners were expected to have a storage life of more than ten years.[108]

The Office of Civil Defense issued food guidelines in June 1964 for federally stocked fallout shelters. Though 1,500 calories consumed per day was determined to be sufficient to sustain daily activity for an individual, the government believed "that healthy persons can subsist for periods up to the maximum anticipated confinement of 2 weeks under sedentary conditions on a survival ration of 700 calories per day." The government considered seven requirements in determining appropriate fallout shelter foods:

> *The food* [should] *be palatable or at least acceptable to the majority of the shelter occupants; have sufficient storage stability to permit a shelf life of 5 to 10 years; be obtainable at low cost; be widely available or easily produced; have high bulk density to conserve storage space; require little or no preparation; and produce a minimum trash volume.*

In light of these criteria, the Armed Services Forces Food and Container Institute chose four items with which to stock shelters: the "Survival Biscuit," the "Survival Cracker," the "Carbohydrate Supplement," and the "Bulgur Wafer." They were packaged separately in sealed cans with an estimated shelf life of between five and fifteen years.[109]

In addition to stocking shelters with food and water barrels, the federal government also stocked each community shelter with a medical kit. Initially developed in the 1962 fiscal year and slightly altered after the 1966 fiscal year, these kits were provided for physical ailments, including emergencies, as well as for "controlling emotional stress." The supplies fell into three categories: "Medication," "Dressings," and "Other." The medication included aspirin, Eugenol, eye and nose drops, isopropyl alcohol, kaolin and pectin mixture, penicillin, petrolatum, phenobarbital, surgical soap, sodium bicarbonate, sodium chloride and sulfadiazine. The dressings included bandages, gauze, muslin, purified cotton and surgical pads. "Other" items included cotton-tipped applicators, tongue depressors, forceps, safety pins, scissors, thermometers and an instruction manual. The general storage life in normal conditions for the items was estimated at a minimum of five years and a maximum of at least ten years, with all of the dressings and most of the "Other" items listed as having an indefinite storage life.[110]

By June 12, 1962, a fallout shelter survey in Denton revealed that twenty-three city buildings offered maximum radiation protection. Office of Civil Defense field operations officer Bill Cox said that Fort Worth firm Freese, Nichols & Endress surveyed Denton, and results showed that the twenty-three buildings were large enough to accommodate at least fifty people and provide adequate radiation protection. One of the buildings was the First State Bank building. Cox, Denton mayor Warren Whitson and bank president W.C. Orr Jr. signed an agreement that month providing the bank basement as a public shelter capable of holding at least 350 people. Two weeks of survival supplies for that number of people would be stored in the basement, including enough food to provide ten thousand calories per person, a quart of water a day for each person, equipment to measure radiation and medical and sanitation supplies. The Freese, Nichols & Endress survey was instigated by the Fort Worth District Office of the Corps of Engineers and was the first of two survey phases in Denton. The firm would also conduct the second phase in Denton and Denton County, beginning in the middle of June, to determine exact number of people that each shelter could hold.[111]

The day after President Kennedy's October 22, 1962 nationwide television address announcing that Soviet missiles were being placed in Cuba and that the United States was implementing a naval quarantine of the island and calling on Soviet leader Nikita Khrushchev to remove the missiles, the *Amarillo Globe Times* published several page-1 Cuban Missile Crisis stories. One referenced the flood of calls to the Amarillo civil defense office for information about fallout, the availability of public shelters and radiation detection equipment and creating in-home shelters. Wesley Williams, director of the Amarillo-Potter County-Randall County civil defense office, told the newspaper that his office had not been this busy since the previous year's Berlin crisis. Williams began fielding calls from concerned citizens at his home Monday night after the president's address, and the following day his office was deluged with similar inquiries. The newspaper listed the fifty-two public Amarillo fallout shelters that met minimum federal requirements and conveyed to readers that they were identified as such by federal fallout shelter signs; a photograph of a sample sign was included on the front page with this caption: "Black and yellow shelter markers will soon be placed on buildings throughout Amarillo, designating structures offering adequate fallout protection and food and medical supplies." The front page also included a photograph of two uniformed men stationed at Amarillo Air Force Base, one donning a holstered firearm and the other holding a telephone receiver, below which was this caption:

> *President Kennedy's message Monday placed U.S. armed forces on worldwide alert. At Amarillo Air Force Base increased readiness and tighter security became evident. Here, Lt. Wensinger, a SAC B52 bomber co-pilot, seeks telephone clearance today to enter the vital SAC unit command post. Airman 2.C. Timothy Hadsell, air policeman, is the armed guard on duty at the entrance to the highly-secret CP of the 4128ᵗʰ Strategic Wing.*[112]

Two days after the president's televised address, the *San Antonio Express* urged citizens to remain calm in light of international tensions centered on Cuba and possible nuclear attack. The city's civil defense coordinator Martin Eser and city manager Jack Shelley encouraged the public to have on hand two weeks' worth of food and water. Shelley also announced that the police headquarters would be the communications center following any disaster. City civil defense siren tests were also discontinued during the crisis, and defective sirens were scheduled to be removed before any false alarms could frighten citizens. City officials also urged locals to learn the signal for an imminent attack—described as "a rising and falling scream of Civil Defense sirens for three minutes"—and to promptly shelter. Downtown businesses were being readied to serve as nuclear fallout shelters, and according to Shelley, other buildings included "the basement of police headquarters, Municipal Auditorium, City Hall, the City Water Board, Market St. station, Central Fire Headquarters and the federal buildings." Since five minutes or less warning time would be available once a Soviet missile was launched from Cuba, Shelley said that evacuating the city in time would be impossible, so residents should not try. Instead, they were encouraged to stock foods at home that did not require cooking, including fruit, Vienna sausage and baby food. Locals were also encouraged to stock disinfectant and deodorant in sanitation containers with lids to avoid unsanitary and unpleasant circumstances at home while sheltering. Though public shelters were available, only about one-third of San Antonio's population could be accommodated by them during the crisis.[113]

The next day, the *Amarillo Globe-Times* announced that the city's October civil defense siren test scheduled for the following day was also canceled, followed by these words from staff writer John Holt: "This otherwise routine news item a week ago would have gone largely unnoticed. Today, the public's awareness of any war threat is nothing to be tampered with." Then he asked this question: "Just what effect has the ominous shadow of impending war clouds produced in Amarillo?" His answers were that civil defense interest had surged, along with calls to the city's civil defense office asking for locations of public fallout shelters. City civil defense director Wesley Williams told the newspaper that about eighty private fallout shelters had been installed in Amarillo. Radio sales had also spiked as people scrambled to learn news of events unfolding in Cuba.[114]

The same edition of the Amarillo newspaper carried an Associated Press story describing actions taken across Texas to prepare for possible nuclear attack, including increased distilled water sales in Houston and Dallas. Dallas grocery stores also had a difficult time keeping coffee, canned foods, powdered milk and other goods stocked. In addition to fourteen days' worth of water, civil defense officials recommended that Texans have two weeks' worth of food on hand; the story suggested "canned meat, fish, poultry, beans, peas and fruits; cereals and tinned baked goods; cheese spreads; peanut butter and jelly with crackers, and evaporated and dried milk." Denton's Leslie T. Holland of the region 5 office told the AP that the U.S. Office of Emergency Planning there had fielded increased numbers of calls from locals seeking information. The Dallas County Red Cross announced that additional first aid classes were being offered, and survival pamphlets were being placed in Fort Worth's city buildings and banks. Dallas public schools superintendent W.T. White announced that district schools were planning more disaster drills. Houston's mayor, Lewis Cutrer, was meeting with civil defense officials from the city, county and state. Eight mayors were taking turns serving around-the-clock shifts in the Jefferson County civil defense headquarters.[115]

The same day, Denton's newspaper reported a similar run on grocery store items there, including "canned goods, bottled water, powdered milk and other non-perishable items since the Cuban crisis began." Toilet paper and paper towels were also in high demand. Office of Civil Defense region 5 public information officer Bill Rosch said that the office had gotten calls from locals seeking recommendations for food and information about fallout and shelters. In spite of the crisis, Rosch said that the regional civil defense office, located on the Texas Woman's University campus in Denton, had not yet implemented any emergency actions.[116]

A companion story in the *Denton Record-Chronicle* also provided information from city manager Homer Bly that residents would be warned of a nuclear attack through local radio broadcasts and a warning siren emanating from the fire tower. Bly also said that amateur radio operators would be enlisted to receive information during a possible power failure, then relay attack warnings through public speakers. The Denton County agriculture agent's office, the Office of Civil Defense Management and Denton's municipal building all offered pamphlets with information for stocking improvised at-home shelters. The story emphasized the responsibility of each Denton family to provide two weeks' worth of supplies for family members. It also listed these "essential supplies: Water in jugs or bottles, a half gallon for each member per day; matches, paper supplies, portable radio, flashlight, candles and holders, first aid kit, blankets, pail, garbage container, games and amusements for the children, personal hygiene needs and can opener." The article also relayed food recommendations for one person for the two-week confinement period:

> *Two packages powdered non-fat dry milk; four cans evaporated milk; two cans each of tomato juice, orange juice and grapefruit juice;…two pounds dried prunes…four of peas, two of corn, two of green beans; and eight cans of assorted soups. Also, two one-pound cans of stew, two one-pound cans of salmon or tuna, four cans of spaghetti and meat balls, two cans of baked beans, two jars of cheese and two of peanut butter, fourteen individual packages of cereal, two boxes crackers and cookies, two jars of instant coffee or tea, two jars instant cocoa, 24 bottles of soft drinks.*

Following these shelter supply recommendations, the story stated that a belowground shelter "with at least three feet of earth or sand above it" provided the greatest fallout protection, though "two feet of concrete will give the same protection."[117]

As the Cuban Missile Crisis ended, the first San Antonio public fallout shelter became ready for occupants. The October 28, 1962 *San Antonio Light* informed readers that Joske's of Texas was the city's first designated public fallout shelter meeting federal requirements. Ceremonies were planned to mark the shelter's readiness, and scheduled attendees included state civil defense coordinator James Garner, Civil Defense Region 5 Office director Bill Parker, Paul Savage from the U.S. Corps of Engineers and state civil defense field operations chief Mattie Treadwell. San Antonio civil defense coordinator Martin M. Eser said that this was one of 170 potential city shelters that could be designated as federally approved and accommodate 121,000 people in an attack. Federal fallout shelter signs were being placed on the exterior and interior of Joske's, and it was being stocked with food, water, radiation detection equipment and sanitary and medical supplies. Civil defense officials emphasized, however, that public fallout shelters were intended only to protect people who were away from home and unable to seek shelter there.[118]

During the Cuban Missile Crisis denouement, the University of Houston student newspaper published a story asking student body members what they would do during an attack. The *Cougar* specifically asked twenty students what their plans were if an attack warning was given while they were on campus, but only three had plans. The newspaper offered this advice:

> *The first thing anyone should do is tune into a Conelrad radio station. Houston area residents will find this station located at 640 or 1240 on the radio dial. The change over from the regular station broadcast takes a few minutes and no alarm should be taken during this time. If possible a container of water should be obtained, a person can live much longer without food than without water. Family and friends should be notified in advance as to your plans.*

The article carried advice from Dean Alan Johnson that students on campus during an attack should seek shelter in a university building's basement if they found themselves unable to evacuate.[119]

Five days later, the University of Texas at Austin student newspaper provided information about where students, faculty and staff could seek

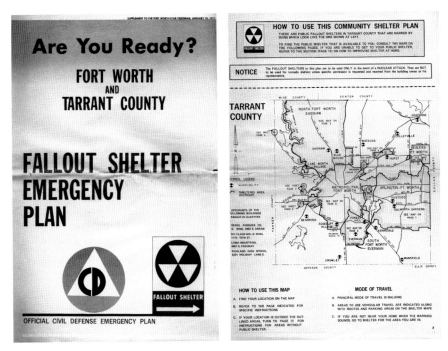

The federal civil defense emergency fallout shelter plan for Fort Worth and Tarrant County. *Civil Defense Museum.*

campus shelter during a nuclear attack. In an article titled "Better Hid Than Dead," the *Daily Texan* conveyed that thirty campus buildings provided a "total of 24,099 safety spaces…2,900 of which will have a 'protection factor' of 100 or better, meaning they would be 100 times better than being outdoors." The university's fallout shelters were also available to the public. Though they had not been marked yet, they were scheduled to be identified as public shelters with federal fallout shelter signs and stocked with supplies, also provided by the federal government. The story pointed out that once a space was identified and marked, it was a public fallout shelter. Travis County housed about three hundred thousand fallout shelter spaces with varying degrees of protection. According to the story, some of the other federally approved "public fallout shelters in Austin are the Austin American-Statesman, the American Legion Hall, the Austin and Driskill hotels, the Capital National Bank Building, the Littlefield Building, the International Life Insurance Company Building, and the Travis County Courthouse." The story ended by calling attention to the timeliness of Austin fallout shelter announcement—available to twenty-four thousand people affiliated

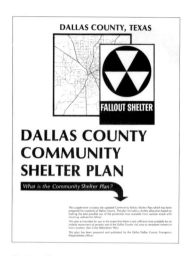

Dallas County community shelter plan. *Civil Defense Museum.*

with the university—after recent fears of nuclear attack during the Cuban crisis, which had ended only a week earlier.[120]

The question of who was responsible for denying entry to anyone seeking shelter during a nuclear attack once a shelter's approved capacity had been reached arose during an early November Amarillo school board meeting shortly after the Cuban Missile Crisis ended. The board designated three schools as public fallout shelters during the meeting—North Heights Elementary School on North Hughes, Margaret Wills Elementary on West 11th and Sam Houston Junior High on Independence—after which superintendent Bob Ashworth asked the question. Amarillo civil defense coordinator Wesley Williams, who also attended the meeting, said that someone must be designated to seal shelter doors during an emergency when capacity was reached. When board member George H. Caulfield Jr. said that he believed people would be unwilling to "play God" and turn anyone away during an attack, Williams responded, "Somebody has to," because capacity was established for each shelter to ensure the survival of occupants for up to two weeks. He also said that the designated person would have to use force—and maybe even weapons—if necessary to turn people away or risk all of the occupants dying. Board president J.W. Collins then said that legal authority would be required to close shelter doors and refuse further admission during an emergency, to which fellow board member Ben H. Stone Jr. replied that the absence of such legal authority was a "weakness" in the civil defense structure. Civil defense director Williams responded that he believed that the federal government lacked jurisdiction to determine who had the authority in such a circumstance and that a city commission should designate with whom the authority resided. He went on to say that he had never been asked the question before and that civil defense planning did not delegate such authority; he would bring up that question at a state civil defense meeting later that month in Austin. Williams also said at the meeting that fifteen Amarillo buildings besides the schools had already been designated as public fallout shelters, and another fifty or so buildings could also provide shelter. He recommended that Sam Houston Junior

Austin American-Statesman. Michael Barera, https://creativecommons.org/licenses/by-sa/4.0/deed.en.

Travis County courthouse. *Larry D. Moore, https://creativecommons.org/licenses/by-sa/3.0/deed.en.*

High could accommodate 140 people, North Heights Elementary 108 and Margaret Wills Elementary 91. Superintendent Ashworth conveyed to the board that administrators were creating an evacuation plan for all Amarillo schools in the event of an attack.[121]

The next month, the University of Texas student newspaper offered editorial criticism of the recent efforts to tag campus buildings with federal fallout shelter signs, telling its readers that "their markings left a lot to be desired," because the yellow-and-black signs, "which are posted near the shelter areas and some of which show protection-seekers the route to fallout shelters are difficult to interpret in several of the buildings." The *Daily Texan* called on local civil defense personnel or university officials to more clearly indicate which campus facilities were fallout shelters: "Under the agreement signed by the University, the Civil Defense office of the federal government was charged with marking the shelter areas. But supplementary markings—or even a widely distributed mimeographed or printed chart of the shelters—would assist interested students, and faculty and staff members, in locating them in advance." The student broadside closed with this rebuke: "Realizing that Civil Defense preparations on the University campus are in their embryonic stages, it must nevertheless be recognized that the present system of identifying fallout shelters is unsatisfactory, incomplete, and confusing."[122]

Another University of Texas student group protested as the Corps of Engineers identified campus buildings competent to serve as fallout shelters. The Austin chapter of the Student Peace Union criticized the process and argued that, based on a recent speech in Austin given by nuclear physicist and Carnegie Institute member Dr. George Hinman, the campus buildings being designated as shelters would not survive a nuclear explosion. In his speech, Hinman said that only structures beyond twenty miles from a twenty-megaton nuclear bomb's explosion could provide adequate fallout protection, and even then, shelters without equipment to provide fresh oxygen for possibly months would also fail. The Student Peace Union criticized the absence of sufficient fallout protection on campus, the inaccurate belief in the safety that ordinary fallout shelters would provide and the increased likelihood that such false comfort would encourage a belief among the general public in unavoidable nuclear war. Austin's being the seat of state government, its housing Bergstrom Air Force Base and its proximity to San Antonio's military facilities were believed to make Austin a high-priority Soviet target during a nuclear attack.[123]

By May 1963, fallout shelter sales in San Antonio had declined dramatically. The city's Housing and Inspections Department issued only nine fallout shelter building permits between October 1962 and March 1963, and most of those were in November immediately after the Cuban Missile Crisis ended. Owners of the fallout shelter companies told the *San Antonio Express* that ignorance, indifference and banks' unwillingness to finance the shelters were the leading reasons that sales had abruptly diminished. The same edition of the *Express* announced that the regularly scheduled test of San Antonio's civil defense sirens would occur at 10:30 in the morning on the following Friday. According to the brief announcement, the city's "sirens are radio operated and such tests must be conducted to ensure all parts being in working order should an emergency arise necessitating their use."[124]

According to the *Denton Record-Chronicle*'s August 27, 1963 edition, a similar sentiment existed there. The absence of an international crisis along with the recently signed limited test ban treaty seemed to discourage locals from making civil defense preparations. Denton city manager Jack Reynolds told the local newspaper that "I'd have to say we don't have a real active [civil defense] program." Of the city's forty-four possible fallout shelters, which could accommodate more than 14,000 people, only thirteen (capable of accommodating 3,491 people) were available for public use, and only six of those (which could hold 1,364 people) were stocked with emergency supplies. Although Denton's two university campuses had a combined thirty-one fallout shelters, none of them were available for public use. During a nuclear attack, the municipal building basement would house the city's emergency communications equipment, though, according to Denton police chief Andy Anderson, the equipment was not there yet. Local radio station KDNT was also able to broadcast emergency directions during an attack. The thirteen public shelters available then were the municipal building, the junior high school, the county courthouse, Jagoe Abstract Company, First State Bank, Denton County National Bank, Denton Federal Savings & Loan, Moore Business Forms Inc., Flow Memorial Hospital, Diesel Power Plant, the municipal water plant, Morrison Mills Elevator and General Telephone Company.[125]

San Antonio's Southwest Texas Methodist Hospital was built with civil defense shelter included. Described as a "survival complex," it was the first of its kind in the nation. Its two belowground levels that served as an extended-stay fallout shelter included all of the necessary medical equipment and facilities to treat wounded patients after an attack. Hospital administrator William D. Hamrick said that the underground portion of the hospital could continue functioning safely insulated from fallout even if the aboveground portion was destroyed by a nuclear blast. "Doctors and nurses who survive the attack could come to the hospital and put it into operation with a minimum of delay instead of having to wait for the erection of emergency hospitals," Hamrick told the *San Antonio Express/News* in September 1963. The hospital could accommodate 1,800 people for more than two weeks after a nuclear attack. The radiation from such an attack, it was believed, would not be able to penetrate the three five-ton doors, reinforced with lead, that would close and seal the area around a thirty-inch wall at the first belowground level.[126]

The University of Houston offered a course that began October 30, 1963, to train architects and engineers to analyze facilities for their possible use as fallout shelters. The fifteen-week course offered by the university was sponsored by the Houston Office of Civil Defense and gave students the opportunity to become licensed. Former Oklahoma State University department of architecture member Arlyn Orr and University of Houston architecture professor Herman Goeters were the course instructors.[127]

Forty professors at the University of Texas (UT) in Austin who were members of a shelter management class spent eight hours during a simulated nuclear attack in the fallout shelter in the business economics building's south basement in early December 1963. Designated communications director O.E. Hinkle relayed that Houston, Fort Worth, San Antonio, Bergstrom Air Force Base and Dallas had also been attacked, and fallout drifting from Bergstrom had reached Austin. Some professors wiled away the time reading or chatting, while others made Christmas decorations. Gladys Hudnall distributed up to a quart of water per shelter occupant, and she served a supper consisting of eight survival crackers to each person as well. Office of Civil Defense field officer Mattie Treadwell evaluated the shelter during the UT exercise, and she said that she believed it was the first of its kind at a large university. Austin–Travis County civil defense program deputy director Carl Bowers and civil defense training and education officer Howard Shackleford taught the shelter management class.[128]

The nation was divided into seven civil defense regions in 1963, and Denton housed headquarters for region 5, yet the city did not have a civil defense organization. That began to change in December of that year when, after learning that the city's two-hundred-bed emergency hospital— along with similar emergency hospitals in more than eighty other Texas cities—would be expanded from offering three days of care to thirty days, the Denton city council voted to start a local civil defense program. City manager Jack Reynolds informed the council that the expanded emergency hospital would require more storage than was available in the city's East Hickory warehouse; either storage would have to be expanded, or Denton would have to end participation in the emergency hospital program. Denton mayor Warren Whitson proposed that the city hire a civil defense director to oversee a full-scale program. Whitson told councilmembers that "during the Cuban situation, people kept calling and asking, 'Where are our shelters?' There was nothing you could tell them, and that was a pretty ticklish situation." Councilman Allen Self agreed that the city needed such a civil defense program: "We don't know what kind of disaster may strike Denton. Few people are willing to admit to themselves that a 150 megaton bomb exploded over Dallas would send its fireball almost to Denton."[129]

Denton's two-story underground federal civil defense facility was unavailable to the public in February 1964, so *Record-Chronicle* staff writer Mike Engleman, who had toured the facility but was not allowed to take photographs, described the complex's interior to the reading public. Deputy regional director of the U.S. Office of Civil Defense Leslie T. Holland told Engleman that the ubiquitous springs that Engleman saw inside were intended to maintain stability during shock waves following a nuclear explosion:

> *In the brightly lighted basement, everything either hangs or sits on springs. Giant heating and cooling systems and power generators squat on heavy springs. Pipes leading to and from the machinery are hinged on springs. And springs, of course, support commodes in the rest rooms.*[130]

The aboveground portion of the facility was actually built to crumble and "blow away in the shock waves of an atom blast." According to Holland, this diminished the risk of debris collecting in front of one of the facility's thirteen-ton lead-and-steel doors to the underground building portion, which would prevent its closing. The subterranean cafeteria could be used to provide a sleeping space, and its storage housed enough food to feed five hundred people for up to thirty days following a nuclear attack. The two belowground floors were described as "made of enough concrete to build a sidewalk from Denton to Downtown Dallas" and was "a complete city for 500. It has everything from a 'decontamination room' equipped with automatic showers to a washer-dryer equipped with laundry room." Only authorized government employees would be allowed inside the complex following an attack. "We can't even bring our families down here," Holland said. "Space is critical. And when an attack comes, we'll need every square inch of it."[131]

A Webb County dual-purpose belowground school and public fallout shelter also made the news in February 1964. Director of the Texas

Department of Public Safety and state disaster relief coordinator Colonel Homer Garrison Jr. praised United High School, about two miles from Laredo, as one of the few schools of its kind in the country and the only one in Texas to be built without federal money. Assistant Secretary of Defense for Civil Defense Stuart Pittman was the keynote speaker at a January 26 dedication event. Unique for the time, the new school both offered air conditioning and served as a fallout shelter. School superintendent H.C. Brantley said that the air-conditioned comfort provided in the harsh south Texas climate had improved student attendance, and its "solid construction, with a 14-inch concrete slab ceiling," eliminated exterior distractions of "jet aircraft, weather disturbances, and outside scenes." Brantley said that "the school is expected to resist obsolescence for 100 years or more." Though the school's gym, auditorium and offices were aboveground, the classrooms and cafeteria were beneath the earth's surface. Designed for 540 students, the school could shelter more than 2,500 people.[132]

Bill Lee of the *San Antonio Light* investigated civil defense indifference in both the city and Bexar County beginning in late January 1965. San Antonio's coordinator of civil defense Martin M. Eser agreed that public civil defense concern had waned. "Public interest in civil defense is about as low now as it has been since I've been in it," Eser, who had worked in the city's civil defense office since its creation in 1957, told Lee. Bexar County civil defense office director C.W. Grantham said that "people generally" had lost interest, though some individuals were still building home shelters. "People are well aware of the world situation, but they like to put off doing something about it, and do something they have a greater preference for." Grantham and Eser both said that public interest in literature available at the county and city offices about home preparedness for nuclear attack had declined, and few booklets were being given away, which was in sharp contrast to the 1962 Cuban Missile Crisis, when they could not keep them in supply. Interest in family survival classes was so low that the minimum number of students to hold a class was rarely reached. Companies that provided home fallout shelters had gone out of business. The only business still listed in the San Antonio phone book that installed fallout shelters was the Farm and Ranch Service Company, but it also provided other services, and its manager, S.A. Pool, told Lee that it had been more than a year since it last sold a shelter. "What the business would require is another Cuban crisis," Lee said. "We must have had 100 or more calls for shelters in those few days—we finally had to quit answering the phone." Eser believed that about 500 family shelters that provided maximum protection existed in San

Antonio, though another 500 to 1,000 offering at least partial protection likely existed. Grantham said that another 250 to 300 family fallout shelters existed in the county beyond San Antonio. He went on to say that interest in family fallout shelters fell by 1963, after the Berlin Wall was erected, the Cuban Missile Crisis ended and the Kennedy administration began a federal public fallout shelter program.[133]

The Potter County courthouse in Amarillo received a commendation from state and national civil defense officials on June 17, 1965, for having installed a public fallout shelter in the courthouse basement. In a written statement, national civil defense director William P. Durkee praised the decision to install the shelter and thereby help the nation "survive and recover in the event of attack." Amarillo civil defense director Wesley Williams also signed the commendation received at the courthouse. The public fallout shelter, which could accommodate 381 people during and after a nuclear attack, had been established three years earlier.[134]

As the Denton Rotary Club speaker on February 3, 1966, Civil Defense Region 5 Director William C. Parker told his audience that civil defense's goal was to provide fallout shelter space for every American. He said that concentrated efforts were being made to find shelter spaces, adorn them with fallout shelter signs and stock them. "Highest priority should go to fallout shelters because the greatest danger is in radioactive fallout during the first hours of an attack," Parker said. He was pleased that Denton had hired a

Potter County courthouse. *Who What Where Nguyen Why, https://commons. wikimedia. org/wiki/ Commons:GNU_ Free_ Documentation_ License,_ version_1.2.*

civil defense director, but he also pointed out that Denton lacked adequate fallout shelters for the population of thirty-eight thousand. The city offered shelter space for only about four thousand people, and most of those shelter spaces were located on Denton's two university campuses. Parker told his audience that although Denton would not likely be targeted in an attack, wind-carried radioactive fallout from nuclear explosions at Dallas or Fort Worth could cover the city.[135]

The University of Houston College of Engineering offered area engineers and architects a thirteen-week course in the spring of 1966 to train them in fallout shelter construction. The course, which met on Saturday mornings for three hours in the Engineering Annex Building, was taught by civil engineering professor Dr. Richard H. Gunderson. According to the University of Houston student newspaper, the course included "basic concepts of nuclear fission and fallout, continuation and natural decay of fallout and environmental conditions in the design of shelters." In addition to learning about fallout shelter design, the students also learned how to construct a fallout shelter within an existing building at little cost.[136]

That June, the San Antonio civil defense office sponsored a nuclear attack simulation, called an "in-shelter exercise." More than one hundred locals participated in the event in the municipal auditorium basement as civil defense sirens sounded when it was time to "take cover." The basement was one of San Antonio's 235 sign-indicated and stocked public fallout shelters. The event lasted from five in the afternoon on a Wednesday until six in the morning on Thursday. At about six o'clock on Wednesday, everyone sheltering in the basement ate a meal of survival rations, which included six crackers, four carbohydrate supplement candies and water. Personnel from all the area military posts aided in the event, which was a component of a thirty-two-hour class to train shelter management instructors.[137]

Southwest Sound Equipment was awarded a contract by the Austin city council on November 17, 1966, to install a "giant voice" public address warning system in the University Tower. The unit was the fifth of its kind to be placed around the city and was scheduled to be 267 feet high and had a price tag of $6,488. The UT student newspaper described the system as a "four horn, 360-degree sound apparatus" that would be installed during the Christmas break. Civil defense coordinator Colonel W.A. Kengla told the newspaper that the tower system was audible just under one-half mile in all directions.[138] The December 2, 1966 edition of the *Daily Texan* announced the next first-Friday-of-the-month morning civil defense siren and "giant voice" test for Austin and listed what those near "the voice" would hear during the

San Antonio municipal auditorium. *25or6to4, https://creativecommons.org/licenses/by-sa/3.0/ deed.en.*

test: "This is a test sponsored by the Outdoor Emergency Warning System. I repeat, this is only a test." The story informed readers that the Tower voice system would be placed there during the first week of Christmas break, when fewer people would be on campus.[139]

When President Kennedy was assassinated in November 1963, space for 110 million shelters had been identified around the nation, of which 70 million were available for use, and 14 million were stocked with supplies. However, the first year of Lyndon Johnson's presidency, Congress appropriated only $105.2 million of the OCD's requested $358 million. By 1968, the final year of Johnson's presidency, the amount requested fell to $77.3 million, of which Congress appropriated only $60.5 million. According to Blanchard, the lack of support for civil defense—caused by the acceptance of the philosophy of mutual assured destruction, the fear that civil defense preparations would actually trigger nuclear war and the prohibitive costs of the Vietnam War— from President Johnson and Secretary McNamara influenced Congress to withhold support as well.[140]

The Cold War ended quietly for the United States in the early 1990s, though, without a nuclear weapon being fired at an enemy. That quiet ending contrasted sharply with the decades of danger, fear and, at times, panic that gripped the nation and Texas in the decades preceding it. This was especially true during the crisis years of the early 1960s as the Cold

Above: Lyndon B. Johnson taking the oath of office aboard Air Force One following the assassination of President John Kennedy in Dallas, November 23, 1963. *www.wikimedia.org*.

Right: Oval Office portrait of President Lyndon B. Johnson, March 10, 1964. *www. wikimedia.org*.

President Lyndon B. Johnson (*right*) speaks with Secretary of Defense Robert McNamara in the Oval Office, November 27, 1967. *www.wikimedia.org*.

War entered its most dangerous period, the apex of which was the Cuban Missile Crisis of October 1962, when the world came closer than it ever has to a nuclear war. Civil defense preparedness became a way of life as the state's communities joined national civilian preparedness efforts to survive a nuclear attack during the Cold War's most dangerous years.

CHAPTER 4

TEXAS MILITARY INSTALLATIONS

T he Cold War saw the birth or expansion of several Texas military installations. Some began during World War II, while the oldest trace their roots to the nineteenth century. All were important to the state and the nation during the Cold War as military personnel prepared to defend the nation against attack or travel overseas in service to the country.

AMARILLO AIR FORCE BASE

Located eleven miles east of the city of Amarillo, Amarillo Army Air Field was activated during World War II in April 1942. The field was created to train personnel to service the B-17, and its first classes began that September; later, B-29 crews were trained as well. The field closed after the war in September 1946. In 1951, it was reactivated and named Amarillo Air Force Base, and it became the nation's first air force base to train mechanics only on jets. Eventually, students there were also trained on the B-47 jet bomber, and by 1955, the base was training five thousand students. A Strategic Air Command wing was added to the base in 1957, and two years later, it was renamed Amarillo Technical Training Center. One hundred thousand students had graduated from the jet mechanic school there by spring 1960. The 3330th Basic Military School arrived there in February 1966, and by the next year, facilities for the school had expanded to 5,273 acres, with more than sixteen thousand personnel. The

Amarillo Air Force Base B-47 aircraft mechanic class, early 1960s. *www.wikimedia.org.*

Amarillo Air Force Basic Training graduation photo, 3332nd Basic Military Training Squadron Flight 495, December 1966. *www.wikimedia.org.*

final class graduated on December 11, 1968, and the base was deactivated at the end of the month. The Texas State Technical Institute's Amarillo branch opened on the grounds of the former military site on September 2, 1970, and the Amarillo Air Terminal also began operating elsewhere on the former base on May 17, 1971.[141]

SHEPPARD AIR FORCE BASE

Sheppard Air Force Base, just north of Wichita Falls in Wichita County, is home to the Eightieth Flying Training Wing as well as the Eighty-Second Training Wing. The United States Army Air Corps created the site as a training facility when J.S. Birdwell sold three hundred acres of land to the U.S. government for $1. Base construction began on June 12, 1941, and was completed the following October. Later, another five hundred acres were added. The base was named Sheppard Field to honor Texas senator John Morris Sheppard, and troops began arriving there to train as medium bomber mechanics and glider pilots. As World War II was winding down in 1945, the field achieved two distinctions—with 46,304 personnel, it became the most-populated American air corps troops site in the world, and it served as the country's only school that trained helicopter pilots. It also operated an air traffic school for military personnel.[142]

After the war ended, the field was temporarily deactivated, and the city of Wichita Falls leased the property, which was used by the National Guard, Midwestern Hospital and Wichita General Hospital. The base was reactivated in 1948, commanded by Colonel Samuel C. Gurney, and it was renamed Sheppard Air Force Base. Eventually the base expanded to cover 5,400 acres, housed thousands of American military personnel, drew thousands of students—including foreign nationals—and grew to employ 2,000 civilians, as it also housed three training schools. The number of base personnel reached 13,861 in 1960. Sheppard AFB began training personnel to operate Titan and Atlas intercontinental ballistic missiles, and eventually, Thor and Jupiter intermediate-range ballistic missile (IRBM) training was added, but all ICBM and IRBM training was discontinued in the middle of the 1960s. From 1960 to 1965, Strategic Air Command stationed an operational wing at the base.[143]

The 3630th Flying Training Wing operated a pilot training program for West Germany and one for helicopter pilots from South Vietnam, and it also operated weather training and aerospace rescue schools there. It was

Sheppard Air Force Base welcome sign, 1962. *www.wikimedia.org.*

renamed the 80th Flying Training Wing in early 1973, and it now provides fighter pilot training for NATO members. In 1966, the Air Force Medical Service School moved to Sheppard AFB, and it was renamed the School of Health Care Sciences in 1971; in 1988 it became the 3790th Medical Service Training Wing. With its population declining as the Cold War ended in the early 1990s, Sheppard AFB underwent downsizing and reconfiguration. The base's Air Training Command became the Air Education and Training Command; Sheppard Training Center became the 82nd Training Wing. The base population of both civilian and military personnel rose to 27,972 by 2005, at which time the base operated an elementary school, bank, base exchange, youth center and theater.[144] In 2019, Sheppard AFB employed 9,576 military personnel and civilians, and it contributed $4.6 billion to the Texas economy.[145]

DYESS AIR FORCE BASE

Tye Army Air Field near Abilene was created in December 1942 but was deactivated after World War II ended. The field was deeded to the city of Abilene in 1947 and used in the early 1950s as the city's airport. In September 1953, shortly after the Korean War ended, construction began on Abilene Air Force Base, a Strategic Air Command site; the base was completed in April 1956. It was renamed Dyess Air Force Base in honor of highly decorated World War II pilot and Texan William Edwin Dyess. The B-47 and KC-97 aircraft there were operated by the first SAC wing at Dyess, the 341st Bombardment Wing. In September 1957, the 96th Bomb Wing began operating there.[146]

The Army operated Nike Hercules antiaircraft missiles nearby, and the Air Force manned Atlas F intercontinental ballistic missiles at twelve sites near Dyess AFB by 1961, though all missile units were deactivated shortly thereafter. The 2nd Air Force assumed control of Dyess AFB in 1965, and the 96th Bomb Wing became the 96th Strategic Aerospace Wing two years later. It operated B-52 bombers with assistance from the 917th Refueling Squadron's KC-135 tankers. Dyess AFB's KC-135s and B-52s flew combat missions in the skies over Southeast Asia between 1965 and 1973. In June 1985, the supersonic B-1B was added to the base, and in 1993, the 7th Wing—four years later becoming the 7th Bomb Wing—replaced the 96th.[147]

The presence of Dyess Air Force Base has been significant for Abilene and Texas in the years since 1942. According to the Texas State Historical Association, the base's economic impact was $307.1 million in 2001, and 5,918 civilians were employed.[148] The Texas comptroller lists Dyess's 2019 economic impact on the state's economy as $3.8 billion, with a total of 6,005 military personnel and civilians employed.[149]

GOODFELLOW AIR FORCE BASE

San Angelo Field, in Tom Green County just southwest of San Angelo, became a U.S. Army Air Corps pilot training base in August 1940 and operated the San Angelo Air Corps Basic Flying Training School. Renamed Goodfellow Field in memory of John J. Goodfellow, a Fort Worth native and onetime San Angelo resident who died while serving in France during World War I, the base began hosting basic training for flying cadets in January 1941 and the Women's Air Force Service Pilots in June 1943. The base was deactivated after World War II but was reactivated in late 1947 under the name Goodfellow Air Force Base and began training pilots for the newly formed United States Air Force. The base's mission transitioned to flight training for B-25 Mitchell twin-engine bombers, but its flight training ended in September 1958.[150]

On October 1, 1958, the base began cryptologic training for students from all of the U.S. military branches. According to the Texas State Historical Association, in 1981, Goodfellow AFB acquired "an additional mission as part of the phased-array radar-warning system, a nationwide network of radar protection against sea-launched ballistic missiles," which would be "one of only four such systems in the continental United States." The base became a "technical training center" in 1985, and the

Seventeenth Training Wing was activated there in July 1993.[151] As of 2019, the base employed 8,309 people and contributed $4.5 billion to Texas's economy annually.[152]

RANDOLPH AIR FORCE BASE

Randolph Air Force Base, northeast of San Antonio, began as Randolph Field, and building it—from 1928 to 1933—was the Army Corps of Engineers' greatest undertaking since constructing the Panama Canal. The Texas Historical Association (THA) describes the base's design, suggesting that the project required five years because of the base's "500-plus Spanish Colonial Revival-Style buildings and the thirty miles of roadways. In the end, the buildings of the base were centered on the field, with the administration building," known as the Taj Mahal, "providing the perfect centerpiece." The THA goes on to explain that the "base streets were laid out concentrically, and the aircraft ramps and runways on the east, west, and south portions of the base formed a square perimeter around the circular layout of the field." The base was named for Texan and Texas A&M graduate William Millican Randolph, who died in a February 17, 1928 airplane crash at Goram Field in Texas.[153]

The Air Corps Primary Flying School began at the base in late 1931, and "primary training" continued for eight years until the school began offering basic training for pilots. Its mission again changed in 1943, and it began training flying instructors. Then, in 1945, the Army Air Force Pilot School replaced the Central Instructors School, and B-29 bomber training was offered. In January 1948, the installation became Randolph Air Force Base, and in March, the 3510th Basic Pilot Training Wing began duties there. Then, in July 1957, Air Training Command moved from Scott Air Force Base to Randolph AFB. Two years later, however, Randolph's Seguin Auxiliary Field opened, but its School for Aviation Medicine was relocated to Brooks Air Force Base. The 12th Tactical Fighter Wing was renamed the 12th Flying Training Wing, which was subsequently activated at the base. According to the Texas State Historical Association, "The wing has served as host for the following headquarters: Air Training Command (now Air Education and Training Command), Air Force Military Personnel Center, Air Force Civilian Personnel Management Center, Air Force Recruiting Services, and the Air Force Management Engineering Agency as well as more than twenty tenant agencies."[154]

Above: Randolph Field
Administration Building,
1938. *www.wikimedia.org*.

Right: Women's Army
Corps personnel,
Randolph Field, 1944.
www.wikimedia.org.

U.S. Army Air Forces North American T-6 Texan training planes passing over the administration building, also known as the Taj Mahal, at Randolph Airfield, 1942. *www. wikimedia.org*.

The administration building, also known as the Taj Mahal, at Randolph Air Force Base, part of Joint Base San Antonio, 2014. *www.wikimedia.org.*

As the Vietnam War ended, the base served a unique function in Operation Homecoming—it offered requalification training for 150 USAF pilots who were returning to the United States after being prisoners of war. This lasted from May 2, 1973, to November 12, 1976. From then until December 1992, the base only offered pilot instructor training. Randolph AFB's 12th Flying Training Wing became part of Joint Base San Antonio in 2010.[155]

LACKLAND AIR FORCE BASE

Though it began as part of Kelly Field, Lackland Air Force Base joined the San Antonio Aviation Cadet Center during World War II in June 1942, and according to the Texas State Historical Association, "It provided classification and preflight training for aspiring pilots, bombardiers, and navigators. By 1945 the base was engaged in the training of personnel for almost every Air Corps need, including fiscal officers, nurses, dentists, medical technicians, psychological research, and a growing enlisted training function." The following year, the site was renamed Lackland Army Air Field in honor of General Frank D. Lackland, one of Kelly Field's previous commanders. Then, in 1948, it was renamed again, becoming Lackland Air Force Base; it gained the nickname "Gateway to the Air Force" because all Air Force personnel were both processed and subsequently trained there.[156]

Training programs for women began at Lackland after World War II, and in 1954, it acquired its first permanent technical training duties with the arrival of the USAF Recruiting Course. The 3275th Technical Training Group also arrived in November 1956 and, with it, air police training. Construction for the Air Force's largest medical facility, Wilford Hall, was completed the following year, and in 1958, the Air Force Marksmanship School as well as the sentry dog training program began there. The Defense Language Institute English Language Center was inaugurated at Lackland in 1966, the same year that the base's size doubled after acquiring 3,500 acres from the Medina Base Atomic Energy Commission.[157]

In 1993, the Inter-American Air Forces Academy began at Lackland so that bilingual base personnel could provide technical training to individuals from the Americas. Later the same year, the Officer Training School left for Maxwell Air Force Base in Alabama. Lackland AFB acquired Kelly Air Force Base's runway and property to its west when it closed in April 2001. Then, in 2010, Lackland merged with Joint Base San Antonio.[158]

Lackland Air Force Base entrance, 1948. *www.wikimedia.org.*

KELLY AIR FORCE BASE

Initially known as Aviation Camp, Kelly Field was named for Lieutenant George E. Kelly, who became the nation's first pilot to die while flying a military airplane when he crashed at Fort Sam Houston on May 10, 1911. The base's site just southwest of San Antonio was chosen in late 1916. Flight training as well as maintenance and supply activity increased with the nation's entry into World War I, which, according to the Texas State Historical Association, brought national recognition:

> *More aviators of World War I earned their wings at Kelly Field than any other field in the United States. At some point of their training most of the future leaders of the air force passed through Kelly Field. They included the later air force chiefs of staff Carl "Tooey" Spaatz, Hoyt Vandenberg, and Curtis LeMay; Charles Lindbergh earned his wings at Kelly Field, as did the famous "Flying Tiger" Claire Lee Chennault. In 1927 the Academy Award-winning movie* Wings *was filmed at the base.*[159]

Eventually pilot training was moved to other bases, and Kelly became identified with the San Antonio Air Materiel Area. During World War II, because so many men entered the military, females made up more than one-fourth of the base workforce. Called Kelly Katies, these women occupied jobs in instrument and electrical repair and sheet metal. In the years following the war, Kelly managed logistics for the B-29, B-36, B-47, B-50 and B-58 bombers; the F-102 and F-106 fighters; and the C-5 transport. The Base Realignment and Closure Commission recommended that the base close in 1995, after which Lackland Air Force Base assumed control of the Kelly Field Annex, along with the runway and nearby property and other base aspects, in April 2001. Kelly AFB closed and became Kelly USA, which became Port San Antonio in 2007.[160] In 2018, Port San Antonio employed 13,364 people, and its economic impact on the state of Texas was $5.6 billion.[161]

LAUGHLIN AIR FORCE BASE

Located seven miles east of Del Rio, Laughlin Air Force Base has undergone a series of name changes. It began as Laughlin Army Air Field in March 1943 and became Laughlin Field in November of that year, then its name was changed to Laughlin Air Force Auxiliary Field before

Above: Laughlin Air Force Base main gate, 1972. *www. wikimedia.org.*

Right: Based at Laughlin Air Force Base, Major Rudolf Anderson Jr. was shot down and killed by a Soviet SA-2 missile during the October 1962 Cuban Missile Crisis. *www.wikimedia.org.*

finally becoming Laughlin Air Force Base. Named for Lieutenant Jack T. Laughlin, the first Del Rio native to die during World War II, the field opened in July 1942 and closed in October 1945, after the war ended. It reopened in 1952 to train F-84 fighter pilots, but it became a Strategic Air Command base in 1957 and operated RB-57 and U-2 aircraft designed for reconnaissance. In fact, U-2s from Laughlin took the photographs comprising the first definitive proof that Soviet missiles were being provided to Cuba and launch sites were being constructed there, which began the October 1962 Cuban Missile Crisis. Laughlin pilot and air force major Rudolph Anderson, whose U-2 was shot down while flying a reconnaissance mission over Cuba, was the only missile crisis fatality.[162] Laughlin Air Force Base employed 3,961 people in 2019 and contributed $2 billion to the Texas economy.[163]

REESE AIR FORCE BASE

Originally called Lubbock Army Air Corps Advanced Flying School, Reese Air Force Base, fourteen miles west of Lubbock, was built beginning in August 1941 on two thousand acres offered by the City of Lubbock. The following November, Lieutenant Colonel Thomas L. Gilbert became base commander. In February 1943, the site's name changed to Lubbock Army Flying School, and it changed again to Lubbock Army Airfield two months later. Following World War II, the base closed with seven thousand pilots having graduated there, but it was reactivated as Lubbock Air Force Base in October 1949 to provide multiengine pilot training. The next month, it was renamed Reese Air Force Base to honor Shallowater native Lieutenant Augustus F. Reese Jr., who died during World War II. The base switched to single-engine jet training in early 1959 and began training international pilots in the 1950s. By 1986, about four hundred students graduated each year, but the base closed shortly thereafter and was renamed the Reese Technology Center. It now houses, among other things, the Texas Tech University Institute of Environmental and Human Health and South Plains College.[164]

Aircraft hangar at the former Reese Air Force Base, now Reese Technology Center, Lubbock, December 16, 2010. *Leaflet, https://creativecommons.org/licenses/by-sa/3.0/deed.en.*

James Connally Air Force Base

James Connally Air Force Base began as Waco Army Air Field, a pilot training school seven miles northeast of Waco, in May 1942. By February 1945, it had become the Army Air Force Central Instructors' School headquarters but was inactivated following the war. The base was reactivated in 1948 as a basic pilot training school, and its name was changed to Connally Air Force Base in June 1949 in honor of Colonel James T. Connally, a Waco pilot who died in Japan in 1945. The base's name changed again shortly thereafter to James Connally Air Force Base, and pilot training ended in favor of training radar operators, bombardiers and navigators. The Instrument Pilot Instructors School, which moved to James Connally AFB, trained instructor pilots from several Allied countries. Officer pilots were also trained as radar operators and navigators to, in the words of the Texas State Historical Association, "provide triple-rated aircraft commanders for the rapidly growing fleet of B-47s"; this training also ended in 1962. The air force was sharing the base with the state of Texas when, in 1965, James Connally Technical Institute (later Texas State Technical Institute) began there. Tactical Air Command gained control of the base in 1966 for headquarters of the Twelfth Air Force. Additionally, General Dynamics Corporation began using the base "as a modification center for the B-58 bomber; the technical center provided many of the technicians for the project," according to the TSHA. The state of Texas purchased the base after the Twelfth Air Force moved its headquarters to Austin's Bergstrom Air Force Base.[165]

Bergstrom Air Force Base

Built in the summer of 1942 on three thousand acres leased from the City of Austin, Bergstrom Air Force Base activated that September seven miles east of town on State Highway 71 as Del Valle Army Air Base. The base's name changed to Bergstrom Army Air Field in March 1943 to honor Captain John A.E. Bergstrom, who was killed in the Philippines on December 8, 1941, the day after the Japanese attack on Pearl Harbor. He was Austin's first World War II fatality. The base's name changed to Bergstrom Field in November 1943, and it finally became Bergstrom Air Force Base in December 1948. Though it originally housed troop carrier units, after World War II, it spent time as a Strategic Air Command base and a Tactical Air Command base and hosted the Twelfth Air Force's headquarters, which oversaw "all Tactical Air Command reconnaissance, fighter, and airlift operations west of the Mississippi River," according to the Texas State Historical Association. Bergstrom Air Force Base closed on September 30, 1993, and Austin voters approved a bond issue that year to build Austin-Bergstrom Airport at the base.[166]

FORT SAM HOUSTON

Fort Sam Houston's construction began in 1876 on the site of a quadrangle more than two miles northeast of the Alamo and was completed two years later. According to the Texas State Historical Association (TSHA), from 1878 to 1879, "the quadrangle was modified to accommodate the headquarters, but the headquarters remained in San Antonio until 1881 when quarters were built for the staff west of the quadrangle on what would be called the Staff Post." The base's largest quarters were built for the commanding general and were named Pershing House for General John J. "Blackjack" Pershing, who lived on the base in 1917. Then known as the post at San Antonio, in 1890, it was named Fort Sam Houston to honor General Sam Houston. Between 1928 and 1939, five hundred buildings were erected there, one of which was a hospital.[167]

According to the TSHA, during World War II, "the headquarters for the Third, Sixth, Ninth, Tenth, and Fifteenth Armies trained and deployed from Fort Sam Houston. So did the VIII Corps, Second Infantry Division, Eighty-eighth Infantry Division, Ninety-fifth Infantry Division, and a host of smaller units. In 1944 the headquarters of the Fourth Army moved into the quadrangle." Among the notable World War II military personnel who had been stationed at Fort Sam Houston were Lieutenant General Courtney Hodges, Lieutenant General Joseph W. "Vinegar Joe" Stillwell and future United States president Dwight Eisenhower. Before rising to the rank of general of the army and supreme commander of the Allied Expeditionary Force in Europe during the war, Eisenhower was chief of staff of the Third Army, stationed at Fort Sam Houston.[168]

The base acquired the new mission of medical training following the war. Brooke General Hospital, which had been built in 1937, became the nucleus of Brooke Army Medical Center. This was followed by the arrival of the U.S. Army Medical Training Center, and in 1946, New York's Institute of Surgical Research, specializing in trauma surgery, was relocated to Fort Sam Houston; the Burn Center was added three years

COLD WAR TEXAS

Fort Sam Houston, San Antonio Quartermaster Depot, circa 1975. *www.wikimedia.org.*

later. According to the TSHA, throughout both "the Korean War and the Vietnam War, Fort Sam Houston trained all of the army's medical personnel and earned the nickname the 'Home of Army Medicine.'" In 1972, the Academy of Health Sciences was formed there and oversaw all army medical training, and the same year, the U.S. Army Health Services Command was created "to command all medical activities in the army," headquartered at Fort Sam Houston.[169]

Fort Sam Houston joined Joint Base San Antonio (JBSA) in 2009, and as the largest of the JBSA bases, it became headquarters.[170] In 2019, Joint Base San Antonio employed 73,707 military personnel and civilians and contributed $41.3 billion to Texas's economy.[171]

FORT BLISS

The federal government established a military site on the Rio Grande near El Paso and ordered the Third Infantry to implement quarters there on November 7, 1848, though it was closed in September 1851. A new post was established on the Rio Grande in early 1854, and on March 8, it was named Fort Bliss in honor of Lieutenant Colonel William Wallace Smith Bliss, chief of staff to General Zachary Taylor during the Mexican-American War and later Taylor's son-in-law. Then, in 1867, a flood destroyed the army post, and troops moved three miles north, where Fort Bliss was reestablished. It was closed in January 1877 but reopened the following year and relocated to downtown El Paso. In 1893, Fort Bliss moved to its final location, five miles east of El Paso.[172]

Fort Bliss transitioned to a cavalry post—the largest one in the nation—and in 1921, the First Cavalry Division was activated. The same year, the Eighty-Second Field Artillery Battalion arrived. The fort experienced massive expansion in the 1940s, growing to more than a million acres and occupying a territory of seventy-five by fifty-four miles. The cavalry transitioned from horses to being mechanized by June 1943, the same year that the First Cavalry Division left, and Fort Bliss became a mostly artillery base. According to the TSHA, "Fort Bliss became an antiaircraft training center in September 1940. German rocket experts, including Wernher von Braun, lived and worked there shortly after World War II." Thus, its Cold War impact was great, according to the TSHA: "In 1946 Fort Bliss became the United States Army Air Defense Center. The base hosted in succession

Fort Bliss, May 5, 1968. *Butch, https://creativecommons.org/licenses/by-sa/4.0/deed.en.*

Fort Bliss Post Hospital, quartermaster general's office, date unknown. *www.wikimedia.org*.

Nike-Ajax, Nike-Hercules, Hawk, Spring Chaparral, and Redeye missiles and other antiaircraft weapons."[173]

A key World War II and Cold War military figure spent his final years at Fort Bliss. General Omar Bradley, who worked closely with Dwight Eisenhower in Europe during the war and served as chairman of the Joint Chiefs of Staff afterward, lived at Fort Bliss from 1977 until his 1981 death.[174] In 2019, Fort Bliss employed 47,045 individuals, and its economic impact on Texas was $25.6 billion.[175]

FORT HOOD

Named for General John Bell Hood, Fort Hood sits on 218,000 acres, most of which are in southeastern Coryell County and southwestern Bell County. Originally Camp Hood, the installation officially opened on September 18, 1942, and continues its original mission of armored training. Upward of one hundred thousand troops at a time were trained there during World War

Fort Hood, World War II temporary buildings, cold storage building, circa 1945. *www. wikimedia.org.*

II, and four thousand German prisoners of war were housed there late in the war. The base's name was changed to Fort Hood in 1950, and demands created by the Korean War required acquisition of 49,578 more acres in 1953. According to the Texas State Historical Association, in "1954 Fort Hood was the nation's only two-division installation"—Second Armored Division and First Cavalry Division—"and the Third Corps was transferred from Camp Roberts, California." Additionally, Fort Hood was headquarters for III Corps, U.S. Army Forces Command, in 1990. The Texas National Guard also operated out of Fort Hood. Several other commands were located there, including the Sixth Cavalry Brigade (Air Combat) and army, marine corps and air force reserve units.[176]

The Second Armored Division was renamed the Fourth Infantry Division (Mechanized) in December 1995. The Texas State Historical Association maintains that "Fort Hood is one of the largest military installations in the world. The primary mission of Fort Hood is to maintain a state of readiness for combat missions, and the dominant activity is the training of III Corps." The base houses elementary schools as well as youth centers and even child care facilities, and its commissary complex is the largest in the country.[177] In 2019, Fort Hood employed 56,023 people and contributed $29.8 billion to the Texas economy.[178]

NAVAL AIR STATION, CORPUS CHRISTI

President Franklin Roosevelt signed a $25 million appropriations proposal for the Naval Air Station, Corpus Christi on June 13, 1940; site construction commenced on June 30, and the station was dedicated on March 12, 1941. The station spans twenty thousand acres across three counties. So many installation facilities had been constructed by 1945 that total costs exceeded $100 million. One of the items built was an eleven-mile permanent military highway with a bridge spanning 1,200 feet across Oso Bay, plus an access road leading to Cabaniss Field. By January 1941, 9,348 people were employed and received $305,125 in weekly payroll.[179]

In its early years, the station was used for pilot, navigator and radio operator training. "In addition, the United States Naval Hospital, the United States Naval School of All-Weather Flight, the Fleet Logistic Air

Mechanic refueling a plane at the Naval Air Base, Corpus Christi, August 1942. *www. wikimedia.org.*

Wing, Acceptance, Test, and Transfer Unit, and the headquarters for the Corpus Christ Naval Reserve Training Center were operating at the Naval Air Station," according to the Texas State Historical Association. Though activity slowed after the war, in 1948, the Naval Air Advanced Training Command arrived at the air station, which also became a permanent U.S. military installation that year. The Blue Angels—the "Navy's precision flight team"—were also relocated to Corpus Christi in 1949 and stayed until 1955. From the 1960s onward, the station "continued to provide fully trained naval aviators of multiengine land and sea planes" and did so through the end of the Cold War.[180] The Naval Air Station at Corpus Christi employed 4,782 people in 2019, and it contributed $2.7 billion to the state's economy.[181]

NAVAL AIR STATION, DALLAS

Located west of Dallas, the Naval Air Station, Dallas began in August 1929 as Hensley Field as a work of the City of Dallas. "The site was leased to the United States Army by the city of Dallas for twenty years for $1.00 a year," according to the Texas State Historical Association, "and the field became the Air Corps Reserve Base in the Eighth Corps Area." When World War II began, however, the lease was extended to forty years. The U.S. Navy began operating there in March 1941, and two months later, it "established a reserve training base on 160 acres adjacent to Hensley Field." On December 23, 1941, less than three weeks after the United States entered World War II, Hensley Field became Midwest Area of the Air Corps Ferrying Command's headquarters. The command became the Fifth Ferrying Group and moved to Love Field. On January 1, 1943, this location became Naval Air Station,

181st Fighter-Interceptor Squadron, F-86D interceptors, Naval Air Station Dallas, 1958. *www. wikimedia.org*

Tactical Electronic Warfare Squadron 34, EA-3B Skywarrior aircraft taxiing, Naval Air Station, Dallas, February 1, 1988. *www.wikimedia.org.*

Dallas, and it provided "primary flight training for naval, marine, and coast guard cadets."[182]

A naval reserve program established itself at the naval air station in Dallas in 1946, and the U.S. Marine Air Reserve Training Command also began there. In September 1949, the navy assumed control of Hensley Field from the air force, yet it continued to train air force reservists. According to the Texas State Historical Association, in "1950 the naval reserve squadron stationed at NAS Dallas was the first air reserve squadron to be called to active service in the Korean War." Beginning in 1952, jets were assigned to the naval air station, and the F8 Crusader was first flown there. The F-14 (Tomcat) and C9B arrived there in the 1980s. The air station in Dallas contributed nearly $76 million to the Texas economy in 1990, and in 1991, 1,700 personnel were deployed to the Persian Gulf.[183]

NAVAL AIR STATION, KINGSVILLE

Originally the Naval Auxiliary Air Station, Kingsville, the site's name changed to Naval Air Station, Kingsville on August 9, 1968. The TSHA provides this information about the station:

Mechanics check engine of aircraft at Kingsville Field, November 1942. *www.wikimedia.org*.

When it was commissioned in July 1942 it was one of three advanced air-training bases of the Naval Air Training Command. At that time its facilities were 85 percent complete; the field did not have a name, being officially designated as "P-4." During World War II four squadrons taught fighter and bomber tactics at the station as well as gunnery for combat aircrewmen. For a short time the field handled an overflow of basic-training recruits from an Illinois naval-training center. At the end of the war pilot training at the base dropped sharply. In September 1946 the station was closed and turned over to the city of Kingsville, which leased the base to the Texas College of Arts and Industries as an agricultural station.

The Kingsville base "was reactivated in April 1951 as an auxiliary air station under the command of the chief of naval air advanced training" at Corpus Christi's Naval Air Station and trained three hundred pilots a year in the mid-1960s. By 1990, the air station was Commander Training Air Wing Two headquarters, "composed of three jet-training wings that trained 170 Navy and Marine Corps aviators each year," according to the TSHA. The station also operates the Orange Grove Naval Auxiliary Landing Field forty-five miles to the northwest of Kingsville.[184] In 2019, the Naval Air Station, Kingsville employed 1,647 people and contributed $852 million to the Texas economy.[185]

NAVAL AIR STATION JOINT RESERVE BASE, FORT WORTH

The military installation that is currently Naval Air Station Joint Reserve Base, Fort Worth was Tarrant Field Airdrome from 1942 to 1943, Fort Worth Army Air Field from May 1943 to January 1948, Fort Worth Air Force Base in January 1948, Griffiss Air Force Base briefly the same month and Carswell Air Force Base between 1948 and 1993. The base was named after Major Horace S. Carswell Jr., and its location was chosen in 1941 for a Consolidated Vultee aircraft factory to make B-24 bombers, with a landing field called Tarrant Field for support. Air force base construction on Tarrant Field's east side was approved in the wake of the December 1941 Pearl Harbor attack, and the Army Air Forces Flying Training Command assumed control of Tarrant Field Airdrome in July 1942. The base's focus changed from training pilots to fly B-24s to B-32s and then again to B-29s in 1945. It became a Strategic Air Command base in 1946, then, two years

XB-52 prototype bomber in 1955 at Carswell AFB, later renamed Naval Air Station Joint Reserve Base Fort Worth. *www.wikimedia.org.*

later, the Seventh Bomb Wing located there received the first B-36, though training on that aircraft was discontinued in 1957. The TSHA provides this information about the base:

> *The Seventh Bomb Wing became operational with the all-jet B-52 and KC-135 in January 1959. The unit was deployed to Guam in June 1965, flew more than 1,300 missions over Vietnam, and returned to Carswell in December 1965. In the 1980s the base received several new weapons systems, including modified B-52H aircraft and cruise missiles. By 1984 Carswell was the largest unit of its kind in the Strategic Air Command. The base contributed personnel and recruits to Operation Desert Storm in the Middle East in 1991.*

The same year, Carswell Air Force Base was scheduled to close, and it did so on September 30, 1993. However, the following October 1, the base became an active Naval Air Reserve Base, and Dallas, Memphis and Glenview Naval Air Stations moved to Carswell, commencing joint reserve operations. One year later, Carswell was renamed Naval Air Station Joint Reserve Base Fort Worth and became the nation's first Joint Service Reserve Base. According to the TSHA, the Fort Worth base "hosts airlift and fighter/attack units from the Navy, Marine Corps, and Air Force reserves," the "assigned fighter aircraft is the F-16" and it "has a post office under the name of Carswell

Base that serves military and civilian personnel…a library, theater, shop, lake and marina, and various recreational facilities."[186] In 2019, the Naval Air Station Joint Reserve Base, Forth Worth employed 6,616 people and contributed $3.7 billion to the Texas economy.[187]

RED RIVER ARMY DEPOT

Located immediately west of Texarkana on government-purchased territory that was once home to more than one hundred farms and ranches, the 1,400 buildings on the Red River Army Depot/Red River Ordnance Depot—which began in August 1941—occupies fifty square miles. According to the TSHA, the depot's "mission is to receive, store, and issue gun-motor carriages, ammunition, explosives, supplies, and equipment for combat vehicles and various types of demolition equipment and supplies for the United States Army Corps of Engineers." The "depot also serves as a major army maintenance point for rebuilding combat and general-purpose vehicles and other types of military ordnance." In April 1943, the installation combined with the Lone Star Ordnance Plant and formed the Texarkana Ordnance Center. "From its activation through December 31, 1945, 2,482,189,387 pounds of material was received, and 1,539,954,000 pounds of material was shipped. In the early 1990s, the base had a small number of military personnel and some 4,300 civil service employees," according to the TSHA.[188] In 2019, the depot employed 3,887 individuals and contributed $1.7 billion to the Texas economy.[189]

Texas has a long and unique history of military service, and this history includes several military installations throughout the state that were key to maintaining the nation's security during the Cold War. One even operated ICBMs as part of the nation's land-based nuclear arsenal. These installations prepared to defend the nation at home and fight abroad. They bolstered the nation's defenses and ensured its safety during a dangerous era.

CHAPTER 5

PANTEX: NUCLEAR STOCKPILE GUARANTOR

Situated seventeen miles northeast of Amarillo in the southeastern portion of Carson County, the Pantex Plant was created on sixteen thousand acres in the Texas Panhandle shortly after the United States entered World War II. The Pantex Ordnance Plant, as it was originally known, began operating in September 1942 to provide bombs for the American war effort. The final of fourteen ordnance plants built in Texas during the war, Pantex generated about four million bombs and artillery shells during that conflict's final three years.[190]

The plant closed the day after the announcement of Japan's surrender in August 1945, and the land on which Pantex was built was leased to Texas Tech University, then known as Texas Technological College, for $1. The federal government, however, leased the land to the university on the condition that it would resume property operations if national security required it. This happened in 1951 when, two years after the Soviet Union successfully detonated its first atomic bomb, the U.S. Atomic Energy Commission reclaimed ten thousand acres of the Pantex property and its facilities. Pantex's Cold War role began as the facility transitioned from conventional bomb production to nuclear weapons assembly. In the words of the United States Department of Energy, the nation's government resumed operating "the Pantex Plant in 1951 and undertook a building campaign to create a cornerstone of the nuclear weapons complex." In 1965, Pantex became the nation's only facility to disassemble and

Pantex Plant sign, September 26, 2013. *www.wikimedia.org.*

modify nuclear weapons, and by 1975, it was the nation's sole warhead construction plant. Operated by the U.S. Department of Energy, Pantex assembled bomb components received from other sites and manufactured nuclear warheads for the nation's nuclear arsenal.[191]

The United States government once moved its nuclear warheads and related materials across the country by train. Between the 1950s and 1980s, "white trains" with reinforced cars and armed Department of Energy sharpshooters poised to fire on any would-be bringers of mayhem transported the nation's nuclear weapons. These trains plodded along their tracks at only thirty-five miles per hour, which resulted in extended transnational trips for their seven-person crews. One popular path found trains moving nuclear weapons from Texas to Bangor, Washington, unloading their nuclear weapons for submarines at Puget Sound. Another oft-used route for nuclear bomb transport was from Texas to Charleston, South Carolina, the location of another submarine base.[192]

Pantex was the hub of this national nuclear transportation network. Since Pantex was the nation's sole nuclear weapons assembler—as it still is—most of the nation's slow-moving nuclear trains traveled through Amarillo. Many of the Potter County seat's residents were Pantex employees then, engaged in nuclear bomb production and disassembly. The *Washington Post* described the site with these words in 1982: "Inside Gravel Gertie bunkers designed to contain explosions and contamination, moonlighting farmers and silent young mechanics bolt together the warheads for Trident missiles and delicately dismantle older weapons."[193]

The trains arriving in Amarillo brought plutonium and uranium, and Pantex was the only site in the country with the necessary facilities—including what *HISTORY* writer Brianna Nofil called "heavily shielded cells"—to unite the materials to create nuclear bombs. Nofil wrote that the Pantex weapons assemblers, "clothed in blue overalls, thick gloves, and safety shoes with rubber slipcovers, worked in pairs to attach the nuclear material and the explosives. From these cells, the bombs were taken to bays where workers would add firing components, casings and tails." Daily trains brought Georgia and Washington plutonium, Tennessee uranium, Florida neutron generators and Colorado bomb triggers to Pantex. The trains were retired in the 1980s, and now the nation's nuclear components and weapons travel on Lockheed Martin trucks.[194]

With its highly sensitive mission, perhaps controversy associated with Pantex was inevitable. In September 1981, the *New York Times* reported on Amarillo Roman Catholic bishop Leroy T. Matthiesen, who was voicing opposition to the recent decision announced by President Reagan to build a new and highly destructive neutron bomb, what Matthiesen called "the latest in a series of tragic anti-life positions taken by our Government." Matthiesen even asked employees at Pantex, where the nation's nuclear weapons were assembled, to resign in protest. None of the 2,400 employees did so, including Robert Gutierrez, a ten-year Pantex veteran and a member of the Catholic church. Matthiesen's request made Gutierrez think through what he did to earn a living, and after months of careful consideration, he concluded that his job caused him to do nothing religiously or morally objectionable.[195]

The United States government was also the defendant in three wrongful death suits stemming from a 1977 Pantex explosion. Employees Chester Grimes, Johnnie Hendershot and Ray Tucker died in a March 3, 1977 explosion during a process called "contact machining" of the explosive LX-09. Relatives of the victims filed suits against the government and asked for damages totaling $750,000. A federal district judge ruled on October 3,

1981, that the federal government was not culpable and ordered those who brought the suits to pay court costs.[196]

Protest over the nation's use of nuclear weapons also resulted in the establishment of the Peace Farm near Pantex. According to its website, the Peace Farm was organized "in 1986 as an information source about the Pantex Plant and to stand as a visible witness against the weapons of mass destruction being assembled there." Though it began as a twenty-acre complex, the Peace Farm currently sits on a single acre adjacent to Pantex on its south side, and because "it is located adjacent to the plant, the Peace Farm has legal and regulatory rights not shared by more distant organizations, and thus plays a unique role in empowering those who would see a world free of nuclear weapons." The website also explains that the organization has hosted educational and religious activities for community members as part of its involvement "in educational, protest and advocacy work on a wide range of peace, social justice and environmental issues."[197]

Of the sixteen Department of Energy weapons production sites around the nation in 1988, Pantex was labeled as the second most dangerous. The same year, asbestos and other dangerous materials required cleanup at the site; belowground gasoline tanks leaked, and other poisonous materials seeped into the soil. With 2,700 employees, the plant was Amarillo's primary employer, and locals forewent pressuring Pantex to implement more stringent environmental protections.[198]

The Cold War ended with the Soviet Union's dissolution in 1991; that same year, the final nuclear weapon was assembled at Pantex. Following a deal with Russia in 1992, Pantex began disassembling warheads. Fearing that local drinking and irrigation water would become toxic, some locals expressed concern for the role that Pantex would play as a plutonium storage site, keeping approximately 110,000 pounds of the radioactive material in underground bunkers. Then, two years later, the site shut down following the inability to locate maintenance records and what the Texas State Historical Association called "a series of safety system failures." Between October 1986 and September 1996, Pantex employees dismantled 12,514 nuclear warheads, and by 1996, the site contained nine thousand plutonium storage pits. The same year, the Department of Energy announced that, as the nation's plutonium storage site, Pantex's number of pits would rise to twenty thousand, and the Amarillo facility would also house the nation's strategic plutonium reserve.[199]

By 2006, Pantex's funding was $513 million, and the facility employed about 3,500 people, which, according to the Texas State Historical

B53 nuclear weapon at the Pantex Plant being dismantled, February 14, 2011. *www. wikimedia.org.*

Association, "included a large paramilitary force team for security at the plant." The TSHA also lists Pantex's total area as 16,000 acres, and "6,000 of those acres were leased from Texas Tech University as a security buffer zone." The entire Pantex site includes "700 buildings, 67 miles of fences, and 55 miles of paved roads."[200] In 2016, Pantex spent nearly $33 million of the $99 million provided for daily operations by its operator, Consolidated Nuclear Security, with small businesses in the Texas Panhandle. That year, Pantex's goal was to purchase 55 percent of its day-to-day needs from small businesses; in fact, it wound up purchasing 88 percent of those needs from small, locally owned Texas businesses.[201]

Begun during World War II to produce conventional bombs for the nation's military, Pantex continued to provide material support for the nation's offensive weapons arsenal through the Cold War. Though it has been the recipient of acrimony as well as the site of protest and tragedy, the Amarillo-area facility bolsters the state's economy as it helps reduce post–Cold War global nuclear weapons stockpiles while ensuring a credible nuclear deterrent for the United States.

CHAPTER 6

MAURICE HALPERIN:
TEXAS-OKLAHOMA COMMUNIST, SOVIET SPY‡

Maurice Halperin betrayed the United States. Having begun his teaching career in Texas in the 1920s, Halperin was a University of Oklahoma professor in the late 1930s and early 1940s when Oklahoma's governor and legislature began actively pursuing Communists in higher education. After Halperin fell under suspicion, he left the university for a job with the federal government's wartime intelligence agency. Still under a cloud of suspicion, Halperin eventually fled the country, never to return. Shortly after the Cold War ended, evidence emerged verifying the allegations made by his accusers that, during the 1930s, Maurice Halperin was a covert Texas-Oklahoma Communist, and during the 1940s, he betrayed his country by committing espionage for the Soviet Union.

Halperin graduated from Harvard in 1926 at age twenty, having studied languages, and he took a job teaching French and Spanish at Ranger College in Eastland County, about eighty-five miles west of Fort Worth. After a year at Ranger, Halperin was accepted to the University of Oklahoma (OU), where he began graduate school in September 1927. Roy Temple House was chairman of the university's modern languages department, and he began a journal dedicated to writing English-language reviews of books that had been written in other languages, *Books Abroad*. Halperin published reviews in *Books Abroad*, and through the journal he was introduced to Marxism, which, he admitted to his biographer, influenced him profoundly:

---

‡ *A version of this chapter previously appeared in Brewer,* Cold War Oklahoma.

Part of the stuff that came in had very distinct Marxist orientations. This was the first time I got literature that had an explicitly Marxist analysis. It was fascinating, a new analytical approach, a new understanding of history....Intellectually it broadened my vision, especially of the contemporary world. Among them, books dealing with the Russian Revolution, which I never would have found on the stands in Norman. An accident, but I think it played a real role in my future development.[202]

With a master's degree from OU in hand, in 1929, Halperin left Oklahoma for the University of Paris to pursue a PhD. While finishing his doctoral work in France in 1931, House offered Halperin a faculty position at the University of Oklahoma. Halperin happily accepted the offer to return to Norman.[203]

During the next ten years in Norman, Halperin studied Latin America, and "at the same time, he began to drift leftward politically," he admitted. In 1932, Halperin attended a speech delivered in Oklahoma City by Communist Party vice presidential candidate James Ford. Ford was Black, and the crowd included both Whites and Blacks. "This was Oklahoma in 1932, and that sort of thing was simply not done there," Halperin said.[204]

Halperin told his biographer Don S. Kirschner that, as a young graduate student at the University of Oklahoma in the late 1920s, he was introduced to the Marxist worldview. Then, when he returned to Norman as a faculty member in the 1930s, he was introduced to Marx himself.

So I started reading Marx....Marx made a tremendous impression and the impression had to do with maybe two or three things. One, his historical method seemed to throw a great searchlight on history. And number two, his critique of capitalism which I got not from Das Kapital, which was just too much for me, but from essays and interpretations by other people. And of course his ethical concerns were expressed in such a convincing way. It was clear that I was dealing with a huge intellect. He was a giant.[205]

Halperin wrote an article about exploitation of Mexican workers in *Current History*, and the article was quoted in a 1934 issue of *TIME* magazine. As a result, he was invited to accompany a group of leftists traveling from New York to Cuba in the summer of 1935 to explore allegations "of atrocities by Cuba's strongman, Batista, in connection with a long-term strike there." When he arrived in his room aboard the ship sailing for Cuba, Halperin saw an issue of the Communist Party newspaper the *Daily Worker*. He said

RANGER

MRS. BONNIE GOODMAN, B. S.
Instructor in Home Economics

MRS. H. M. NICHOLS, B. A.; M. A.
Professor of Spanish

MAURICE HALPERIN, B. A.
Professor of French

NORMA WOODIE GRAHAM, B. A.
Professor of Latin

Ranger College 1926–27 yearbook photographs of faculty members, including Maurice Halperin. *Author.*

that he then realized that the fellows traveling with him were more than just fellow travelers. "So I could see some element of the Communist Party was involved in this thing," he told Kirschner.[206]

The trip to Cuba, including a brief detention of the ship's passengers by Cuban police, was chronicled by passenger and leftist playwright Clifford

Odets in the Marxist magazine *New Masses* shortly after the group returned to New York, and word of the detention quickly arrived in Oklahoma. Just as quickly, University of Oklahoma president William Bizzell summoned Halperin to his office to explain his role in the affair. Bizzell reminded Halperin of the need for a good public image and ended the meeting without taking any action.[207]

The trip to Cuba among Communists put Halperin in the company of people with whom he increasingly shared a worldview. In the 1930s, he wanted the Democratic Party to oppose fascism in Europe, which caused him to support the foreign policy of the Communist Party USA. A supporter of FDR's New Deal domestically, by 1936 he was, by his own admission, a fellow traveler. For two years beginning in the fall of 1937, Halperin regularly contributed to a faculty column, the "Faculty Forum," in the University of Oklahoma's student newspaper the *Oklahoma Daily*. He wrote mostly about the Roosevelt administration and world events, especially overseas fascism. Because the Soviet Union opposed fascism, Halperin gave Soviet leader Joseph Stalin a pass when the purge trials in the Soviet Union found innocents admitting guilt in supposed plots to undermine the Soviet government. Stalin, he wrote, was preferable to his fascist counterparts. However, when the Nazi-Soviet Pact was announced in 1939, Halperin went strangely silent and devoted no column inches to the alliance. He also chose not to comment on the September 1939 Soviet invasion of Poland and the subsequent invasion of Finland. Then, in 1940, he stopped writing his column altogether.[208]

In 1938, Halperin made a financial decision that would haunt him for years afterward. He spent hundreds of dollars on Soviet bonds from the Chase Manhattan bank to earn the 7 percent interest that was advertised, which was more than twice the yield of American bonds at the time. Then, after the Nazi-Soviet Pact in 1939, Halperin decided to sell the bonds. Chase Manhattan sent the money to Halperin's bank along with paper notification to pay him that amount. Suspicious, the bank notified the FBI and University of Oklahoma president William Bizzell. According to Halperin, he was accused of being a Soviet spy, though nothing came of the incident then.[209]

In January 1939, Oklahoma governor Leon Phillips claimed that professors at the University of Oklahoma in Norman were teaching communist ideology, and he called for the firing of those professors. Phillips's accusations led many associated with the University of Oklahoma to call for an investigation. Professors there believed Phillips's claim of subversives in their midst was based on participation by some faculty members in both the state's Federation for Constitutional Rights and a state civil rights symposium.[210]

During the Oklahoma legislature's first week in session, House Bill 17, prohibiting Communist Party members from appearing on state ballots, was passed by the full house 118–0. However, the Oklahoma Federation for Constitutional Rights insisted the bill receive a public hearing. Unhappy with the state legislature's aggressively attempting to curb the rights of perceived subversives in early 1941, leaders of the Oklahoma Federation of Constitutional Rights, one of whom was Halperin, forced a showdown with the legislature. Halperin maintained that the federation did not intend to uphold Communism but instead to protect the political rights of all Oklahomans. At the end of January, state senator Joe Thompson introduced legislation to begin investigating the Communist Party in Oklahoma.[211]

The Senate Committee on Privileges and Elections, tasked with the Communist investigation, met for the first time on February 4, 1941, and seven University of Oklahoma faculty members were among the thirty-five individuals subpoenaed to testify. Governor Phillips was the first to take the stand, and he announced during his testimony that he had provided the FBI several documents concerning Oklahoma Communism in the previous two years. Oklahoma's "Little Dies Committee" heard witness testimony throughout February. Testifying before the committee on the final day were University of Oklahoma philosophy professors Charles Perry and Gustav Mueller, education professor John Bender, and modern languages professor Maurice Halperin.[212]

During his testimony, Halperin was asked if he knew any Communists, and he answered that he did not. He was asked if he was a Communist or had attended any Communist Party meetings, and he again answered negatively. He also denied that he "believe[ed] in the Russian cause." Then the committee asked about the 1935 trip to Cuba, and as Kirschner relates, "his replies were more than a bit disingenuous." When asked the purpose of the trip, he said "to study the culture, the civilization and the political situation in Cuba." In response to a question about being arrested, "he replied that they had been 'detained,' and explained that the authorities 'preferred we did not land because the situation there was rather tense. They feared for our safety.'" This was untrue. Additionally, though Halperin was asked who accompanied him on the trip, he failed to mention the Communist presence among his fellow travelers.[213]

After the investigation was concluded, the Little Dies Committee reported its findings to the whole senate on May 7, 1941, asserting that the Communist Party was "active in the state and engaged in the field of propaganda and agitation," that more than thirty local Communist Party chapters existed, that total party membership exceeded one thousand, and that "Communists worked in all sections of the state." One of the committee's eleven recommendations was that the University of Oklahoma fire Maurice Halperin.[214] The issue was resolved, however, when Halperin accepted a job with the Office of Strategic Services (OSS), the forerunner to the Central Intelligence Agency, as a Latin American analyst.[215]

In 1946, amid souring relations with the Soviet Union, Congress received information about Communists in the OSS. One intelligence official singled out was Maurice Halperin. Aware of the allegation, Halperin decided to leave the OSS and take a job representing the American Jewish Conference to the United Nations. One morning that same year, Halperin read in Drew Pearson's newspaper column that he faced indictment for espionage while with the OSS. Though startling, nothing came of this public allegation.[216]

Why wasn't more done by the U.S. government in light of the espionage allegation? In a word, laxity. Halperin wasn't the first American government official accused of spying without repercussions. In 1939, Laurence Duggan of the State Department was told by Undersecretary Sumner Welles that State had information that Duggan had passed classified department documents to a Soviet agent. Instead of being fired and prosecuted, Welles told Duggan to seek employment elsewhere. Not only did Duggan not leave the State Department, but he was also later named Secretary of State Cordell Hull's personal advisor. This allowed Duggan to continue spying for the Soviet Union during World War II.[217]

The American security laxity was influenced by both naivete and the pressing issues of war. According to Katie Marton, author of *True Believer: Stalin's Last American Spy*, Communists in the 1930s and '40s were seen by some "as just a bunch of youthful radicals posing no danger to anyone at home or abroad." And the OSS was just as blind to the dangers of Communist espionage as the State Department was during the war years. The director of the OSS was William "Wild Bill" Donovan. Though he later became intensely anti-Communist, during World War II he was unconcerned where intelligence came from if it helped beat the Germans. Donovan once said that "I'd put Stalin on the OSS payroll if I thought it would help us defeat Hitler." He also "claimed that leftists were often the bravest spies and saboteurs." As Donovan put it, "Every man or woman who can hurt the Hun is okay with me."[218]

Even FBI director J. Edgar Hoover seemed unconcerned about the possibility of Communists with malign intentions penetrating the American government. Though aware of J. Peters, Hoover paid scant attention to the man who operated the Ware Group, an underground Communist group of New Dealers that included Alger Hiss, Nathaniel Weyl, Laurence Duggan and more than thirty-five others in Washington, D.C. By the late 1940s, Hoover regretted his inaction early in the decade. "Partly to compensate for his prior negligence, Hoover ignited a witch hunt long past when the witches were dead," Marton wrote. "In the early to midthirties, however, they were very much alive."[219]

So the OSS wasn't the only government agency that turned a blind eye to Soviet agents in its midst. Because of the blindness toward Soviet intentions during the 1930s and 1940s within the State Department, the FBI and the OSS, Halperin was allowed to walk away from the nation's wartime intelligence agency after having been accused of espionage, and nobody batted an eye. The national feeling toward Communists in government would soon change, though, and 1950s America would prove to be much less hospitable toward Soviet sympathizers.

Halperin left the American Jewish Conference to take a job with Boston University in the Latin American regional studies department. While in Boston, Halperin's life changed dramatically in 1953. In the era of McCarthyism, the Senate's Internal Security Subcommittee (SISS) named as its chair Republican senator William Jenner, who investigated suspected Communists. These hearings found several professors asserting their Fifth Amendment right against self-incrimination during testimony, for which they were fired from their universities. Halperin was subpoenaed, and in March 1953, he testified before the Jenner Committee. Asked if he had been a member of the Communist Party and if he had engaged in the kind of espionage activity that former Soviet spy-turned-informant Elizabeth Bentley had accused him of to the FBI and the House Un-American Activities Committee (HUAC), as well as being asked about his political activities at the University of Oklahoma, his Cuba trip, the Soviet bond purchase and other matters, Halperin generally invoked the Fifth Amendment, though he did assert that he did not commit espionage.[220]

Shortly after Halperin's testimony, Nathaniel Weyl, an admitted former Communist, also testified before the Jenner Committee. A New York City Communist, Wyle took a job in Washington, D.C., in 1933 in the federal Agricultural Adjustment Administration (AAA). According to Kirschner, while with the AAA, Hiss "joined a secret Communist party cell, most of whose members were later identified by Whittaker Chambers. He left the New Deal in 1934 to work full time for the Communist party by organizing farm workers in the Midwest." Weyl testified that he learned of Halperin through Homer Brooks, who had worked as an official for the Communist Party in the American Southwest. Brooks told Weyl of Halperin's having "been 'accredited' as the Texas-Oklahoma representative of the Communist party to the Mexican Communist party." Even Halperin's biographer concedes that Weyl was credible. The former Communist's testimony supported charges that Halperin had been a Communist while a professor at the University of Oklahoma, his protestations to the contrary before the Sooner State's Little Dies Committee notwithstanding.[221]

In the fall of 1953, a story broke that drove Halperin from both Boston and the United States when, for the second time, he was publicly linked to espionage. This time, the accusation came from high officials in the federal government. On November 17, President Eisenhower's attorney general, Herbert Brownell, testified before the Jenner Committee and read a November 1945 letter from FBI director J. Edgar Hoover to President Truman "identifying a spy ring that had been functioning in Washington during the war." The substance of the letter came from a deposition provided to the FBI by Elizabeth Bentley, and Halperin was one of the spies named. The director of the FBI, through the attorney general of the United States, using correspondence that included the president of the United States, claimed that Maurice Halperin was guilty of espionage on behalf of the Soviet Union.[222]

The next day, Wednesday, November 18, 1953, Boston University suspended Halperin, pending a university committee meeting the following week to clarify the issues in which he was involved. One week after his suspension from Boston University, Halperin and his wife, Edith, purportedly fearing for his job and his ability to gain other American employment should he be fired in such an uncertain political environment, left Boston for Mexico. If Halperin had been liaison to the Mexican Communist Party as the Texas-Oklahoma representative of the Communist Party USA during the 1930s, as Nathaniel Weyl had testified, Halperin would have had contacts there.[223]

Maurice Halperin's life changed dramatically when Elizabeth Bentley accused him of being a spy for the Soviet Union. He denied her allegations, just as he had denied being a Communist in testimony before Oklahoma's Little Dies Committee in 1941 and before the FBI in 1942 and 1947, yet he fled the United States and, in the words of his biographer, "spent years of exile in Mexico, the Soviet Union, and Cuba, before settling in Canada." Either Bentley lied or Halperin lied.[224]

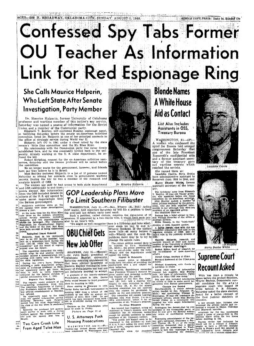

The Sunday Oklahoman, August 1, 1948. *Author*.

As Kirschner points out, Elizabeth Bentley joined the Communist Party in the 1930s, and she began working in "its underground apparatus in New York" by decade's end.[225] She answered to Jacob Golos, with whom she became romantically involved. Golos worked for the NKVD, a predecessor of the Soviet Union's KGB. During World War II, she made contacts with employees of multiple government agencies in Washington, D.C. After Golos died in 1943, she became leery of her NKVD superiors, and she became paranoid that the FBI would soon arrest her for espionage, so in late 1945, she went to the FBI and confessed. According to Halperin's biographer,

> *She testified behind closed doors for a grand jury in 1947 and before two congressional committees (including HUAC) in July 1948, when her revelations became public knowledge for the first time. Eventually she named more than one hundred people, but subsequent investigations focused primarily on the more than two dozen who were still employed by the federal government when she began to talk to the FBI in 1945. One of them was Maurice Halperin.*[226]

Bentley claimed that Halperin had been a member of the Communist Party when he lived in Oklahoma in the 1930s. She said that when Halperin arrived in Washington, D.C., after taking the OSS job, he and former University of Oklahoma colleague Willard Park contacted Bruce Minton of the leftist *New Masses* magazine "and told him that 'they desired to be placed in contact with some Communist in the East.'" Minton took this to Golos, who put them in touch with Bentley. She said that she first met with Halperin late in 1942 at Willard Park's home in Maryland, "at which time she 'arranged to collect Communist Party dues' from him." Shortly thereafter, "Golos went to Washington 'and apparently made arrangements with them on that occasion to be supplied…with certain information to which they had access in their respective offices.'"[227]

Bentley said that Halperin "passed along 'mimeographed bulletins and reports prepared by OSS on a variety of topics and also supplied excerpts from State Department cables to which he evidently had access.'" FBI files also included a letter from within the bureau to Director J. Edgar Hoover discussing this information, saying "that in Bentley's early contacts with Halperin 'he had apparently unlimited access to what she describes as daily cabled intelligence summaries compiled by the State Department.'" Bentley visited Washington every two weeks, and this letter states that "HALPERIN would have a two-weeks accumulation of such summaries and sometimes would turn them over physically to her, while at other times he would perhaps clip out a pertinent paragraph or two and hand it over to her." Bentley also said that after OSS security was tightened, Halperin was forced to take greater care not to be discovered conveying this information to her, so he "adopted the practice of personally typing digests of such information as he thought of interest."[228]

Bentley told government officials that Halperin would occasionally come to New York, where she and Golos would spend the evening with him dining and enjoying a show. She conceded that Halperin may have believed that the classified OSS information he was giving to her was destined for the Communist Party USA instead of the Soviet Union, though the law did not recognize a distinction. The Espionage Act of 1917—under which Julius and Ethel Rosenberg were convicted in 1951 and subsequently executed in 1953—outlawed transmission of classified documents to unauthorized personnel, which means that if Bentley's allegations were true, Halperin violated the Espionage Act. After their last interaction in 1944, Bentley was told by a Soviet contact that OSS director William Donovan confronted Halperin about being a spy, after which Halperin no longer met with his Soviet intelligence contact, and she lost track of him.[229]

Kirschner summed up Bentley's allegations against Halperin:

She had firsthand knowledge that Halperin was a member of the Communist party; that he paid party dues to her; that he passed along printed material from the OSS and the State Department from late 1942 or early 1943 until late 1944, approximately two years; and that he occasionally met her and her superior in New York City. She had hearsay information that it was he who had initiated the contact with Communists in Washington; that the material he gave to her was prized by the NKVD; and that Donovan was aware of Halperin's activities by 1945, and had confronted him with them. She also knew that Halperin had been at Oklahoma University, that Willard Park had been there with him, and that Park was now employed in Washington.[230]

From 1940 until 1949, the FBI kept a file on Halperin, though little in it backs up Bentley's allegations. The file includes a May 1940 allegation from an anonymous Norman source noting that Halperin was "a suspect in 'espionage and Communistic activities.'" Hoover notified the FBI's Oklahoma City office when Halperin went to work for the federal government in Washington in 1941, pointing out that he had been accused by many in Norman of having Communist beliefs. In February 1942, the FBI's Washington office questioned Halperin under oath, and he swore that he had never been a Communist Party member. This echoed his testimony the previous year to the Oklahoma Little Dies Committee.[231]

In his 1953 testimony before the Jenner Committee, Nathaniel Weyl said that the Communist Party organizer for Texas and Oklahoma, Homer Brooks, told Weyl that Halperin was a Communist. Halperin told his biographer that he had never heard of Homer Brooks. In 1993, however, Weyl provided further information to Kirschner that he had not provided in his 1953 testimony, including details involving his late wife, Sylvia. Weyl informed Kirschner by letter that, in the 1930s, Sylvia had

accepted the job of organization secretary (the no. 2 spot) of the Texas-Oklahoma district of the CP. When we went down to Mexico, Homer told her to take over Halperin's job as rep to the Mexican Party. She met with Halperin at our hotel. I seem to recall meeting him then, but was not present at her talk with him. She told me that he had been uncooperative and resentful at having been replaced.[232]

In a follow-up telephone conversation, Weyl said that the meeting with Halperin was in 1936 or 1937. In his letter to Kirschner, Weyl wrote that even if Halperin was not a "card-carrying" Communist Party member in the 1930s, that distinction was irrelevant, because "the criterion for the communist movement at that time was not whether one carried a membership card," because neither of the Weyls did, "but whether or not one accepted the discipline of the party and understood its ideology and line. If Dr. Halperin says he was never a party member, this may be a semantic issue without too much substance." After Kirschner confronted Halperin with this information during the writing of the biography, Halperin claimed that though he had met Nathaniel Weyl while in Mexico conducting journalistic research, he never met Sylvia, and he was not a representative to the Mexican Communist Party. However, Halperin had previously told Kirschner that he had, in fact, met Sylvia Weyl then, in Mexico. Whether Halperin was mistaken or lying, former Communist Nathaniel Weyl implicated Maurice Halperin in 1953 and again forty years later as a Communist and the leader of the Texas-Oklahoma Communist Party during the 1930s, while Halperin was a faculty member at the University of Oklahoma.[233]

Unfortunately for Kirschner, he did not have the benefit of information provided by Venona when he published his biography of Halperin. Venona was the name of a top-secret American program begun late in 1943 to decipher encrypted messages sent from Soviet diplomats in the United States to Moscow. Its hidden fifty-year existence was revealed to the American public in 1995. According to historians John Earl Haynes and Harvey Klehr, these deciphered messages showed that the Soviet Union, though a wartime ally, had, since 1942, placed at least "349 citizens, immigrants, and permanent residents of the United States" as spies in the American government and military, including the Manhattan Project. Spies such as Assistant Treasury Secretary Harry Dexter White and presidential aide Lauchlin Currie were highly placed American government officials. Another was Maurice Halperin. According to Haynes and Klehr, Venona shows that Halperin, while employed with the OSS, "turned over hundreds of pages of secret American diplomatic cables to the KGB."[234]

Venona corroborates Elizabeth Bentley's description of Halperin's espionage productivity. Halperin specialized in providing Soviet intelligence with "sensitive dispatches that were furnished to the OSS." In all, twenty-two decoded Venona messages detail Halperin's participation in espionage for the Soviet Union. According to Haynes and Klehr,

Halperin handed to the Soviets U.S. diplomatic cables regarding Turkey's policies toward Romania, State Department instructions to the U.S. ambassador in Spain, U.S. embassy reports about Morocco, reports from Ambassador John Winant in London about the internal stance of the Polish government-in-exile toward negotiations with Stalin, reports on the U.S. government relationship with the many competing French groups and personalities in exile, reports of peace feelers from dissident Germans being passed on by the Vatican, U.S. perceptions of Tito's activities in Yugoslavia, and discussions between the Greek government and the United States regarding Soviet ambitions in the Balkans.[235]

In addition to compiling diplomatic information for Soviet sources, Halperin also slanted OSS reports to favor the Communist perspective.[236]

Halperin's inconsistent answers about Sylvia Weyl were not the only contradictory answers that he gave his biographer. Halperin told the FBI in 1947 that he was not a Communist, had never met Elizabeth Bentley and had never communicated with Soviet intelligence agents. Yet Halperin told Kirschner in the 1990s that he *had* met with Bentley but only in her capacity as assistant for Earl Browder, head of the Communist Party USA, and he never passed classified documents to her.[237]

Soviet intelligence gave code names to their American assets and used those names in their communications. Halperin's code name was "Hare," and it was included in a November 23, 1945 message from Moscow listing thirteen agents with whom Anatoly Gorsky, a Soviet agent working in the United States, was to discontinue contact because of Elizabeth Bentley's confession of Soviet espionage to the FBI earlier that month.[238]

The U.S. government was unwilling to reveal the existence of Venona, so prosecutors pursued cases against spies in the 1940s and 1950s without the program's information. Without corroborating evidence, the government was often unable to bring those named to trial, much less get a guilty verdict. According to Haynes and Klehr, "Four of those Bentley named did testify, denied her charges, but then put themselves beyond prosecution for perjury by leaving the United States," including "Duncan Lee, Frank Coe, and Lauchlin Currie." The fourth was Maurice Halperin. Though Maurice Halperin denied Elizabeth Bentley's allegations about his involvement with Communism and Soviet espionage, Venona—which implicated Julius and Ethel Rosenberg, Harry Dexter White and Alger Hiss, among many others, in Soviet espionage—shows that Bentley told the truth and Halperin lied.[239]

Maurice Halperin swore under oath in the 1940s and 1950s that he was not a Communist, that he had never met Elizabeth Bentley and that he had never made contact with any Soviet intelligence agents or spied for the Soviet Union. Bentley and Nathaniel Weyl, on the other hand, testified that Halperin was a Communist in the 1930s while he was a University of Oklahoma professor, and Bentley testified that he later engaged in espionage for the Soviet Union. Forty years later, Weyl reaffirmed to Halperin's biographer his previous testimony that Halperin was a Communist and asserted that the former Ranger College professor had also been the Texas-Oklahoma Communist Party representative to the Mexican Communist Party during the 1930s. Despite Halperin's denials in sworn testimony and to his biographer, Venona confirmed Halperin's Communist activity and Soviet espionage. Even if the search for Communists in Texas, Oklahoma and the nation was largely a baseless witch hunt—though Venona suggests that that assessment may deserve some reevaluation—Halperin's case is an example of the aphorism that even a broken clock is right twice a day. Maurice Halperin was exposed as a Texas-Oklahoma Communist who became a Soviet spy.

CHAPTER 7

COLD WAR LEGACY§

The Cold War ended when the Soviet Union dissolved in 1991. That conflict between the United States and the democratic West against the Soviet Union and its satellites behind the Iron Curtain lasted more than four decades and left its imprint on the entire nation, including Texas. With the introduction of nuclear weapons, the Cold War became increasingly dangerous as the world's two superpowers sought to defend themselves and advance their interests. According to Scott D. Hughes in *Encyclopedia of the Great Plains*, "As the ideological battles played out, technological advances in weaponry increased the threat of thermonuclear holocaust."[240]

Just three years after World War II ended, the Strategic Air Command (SAC) made Offutt Air Force Base near Omaha, Nebraska, its headquarters. "SAC served as the air arm of the nation's offensive strategy for waging nuclear war," wrote Hughes, "and it existed as an icon of American military power for the duration of the" decades-long Cold War. SAC expanded its presence in the middle of the country with "longrange bombers, such [as] the B-36 and B-52, planes that were capable of deployment into Soviet airspace." These bombers were supplanted in importance by intercontinental ballistic missiles such as the Atlas, which was deployed near air force bases in states that included Oklahoma, Texas and Kansas. These military installations and the missile sites attached to them "served as economic engines, providing well-paid and secure civilian support employment to local inhabitants in host communities."[241]

---

§ *A version of this chapter previously appeared in Brewer,* Cold War Oklahoma.

As discussed in chapter 2, though economically advantageous for the states and localities that built ICBM sites and housed the missiles and militarily advantageous for the nation in defending it and deterring possible attack, building those sites was dangerous. More than fifty people died while building ICBM sites across several states, including five who died building Texas Atlas missile launch sites.

Three employees died in an explosion at the Amarillo Pantex Plant.

Americans also died while fighting hot wars to stop Communist aggression in Korea and Vietnam. Of the more than 36,000 Americans who died fighting in Korea, 1,779 were from Texas.[242] Of the more than 58,000 Americans who lost their lives serving the United States in the Vietnam War, 3,415 were from Texas.[243] Though the United States was never officially at war with the Soviet Union during the Cold War, that conflict inspired American involvement in war abroad and defense at home that cost thousands of American lives. For the loved ones of those Americans—including Texans—who, in the enduring words of General Douglas MacArthur, "gave all that mortality could give," the loss is part of the Cold War's legacy.[244]

The economic cost to the nation and its taxpayers was also high. According to *Encyclopedia of the Great Plains*, "By 1995, the costs associated with the cold war [*sic*] had exceeded $5 trillion."[245] Defense contractors, half of the "military-industrial complex" that President Eisenhower warned the nation of during his January 1961 farewell address to the nation, benefited enormously.

Another aspect of Texas's Cold War legacy includes the discarded Nike Hercules antiaircraft and Atlas F intercontinental ballistic missile launch sites. Some of the Nike sites became the property of private individuals; others were transitioned to use by school districts, and still others were adapted for other military use. All the Atlas sites were sold after the program was phased out in 1965. Some are owned by private individuals, while school districts own others.

Anyone willing to pay the asking price would likely be able to buy an abandoned ICBM launch site. In 2017, an Atlas F complex in New York was listed for sale. In 1997, it was purchased for $160,000, but in 2015, it was sold for $575,000. The 2017 asking price was $3 million. An Atlas site near Topeka, Kansas, was sold in the 1980s for $48,000, and the 2017 asking price was $3.2 million.[246] The 2022 asking price for the Abilene, Kansas, Atlas missile site was $380,000, down from $420,000 two years earlier.[247]

As the nation implemented civil defense measures to survive a nuclear attack, Texans sprang into action. Public fallout shelters were identified and stocked, home shelters were built and local civil defense units formed and planned for the unimaginable. College campuses prepared to survive nuclear attack. Civil defense preparedness, like nuclear deterrence, also cost. In the words of Hughes, states like Texas "emerged from its cold war [*sic*] experience with deep ties to the federal defense budget, and with fallout shelters now used for storing canned goods and for refuge from tornadoes."[248]

The Cold War ended without a nuclear holocaust endangering civilization. As with any event that fades with the passing of time, the Cold War is a distant memory to some and nothing more than an era only known through history books by those too young to remember. It was, however, a dangerous time for Texas, the nation and the world. Fortunately, through the leadership of Presidents Eisenhower, Kennedy and others, nuclear war was averted more than once, as rational leaders chose peace over war and life over national death in several crises. Our task is to remember the sacrifices, the stakes, the failures and the successes—to learn from our past as we chart our future.

The Cold War began with uncertainty. Nobody knew how long it would last and if it would end peacefully or amid the ruins of a nuclear conflagration. The American foreign policy that guided the nation through the Cold War was begun under President Truman and, in large measure, continued by all subsequent Cold War presidents, Democratic and Republican. Having lived through the entire Cold War, Clark Clifford, former counsel to President Truman, wrote these words about that policy in the early 1990s: "The policy that truly succeeded was born…when, in less than three years, President Truman unveiled the Truman Doctrine, the Marshall Plan, [and] NATO." Then, in the course of "the next forty years, the essential core of President Truman's policies survived…the four great challenges of…the Korean War, McCarthyism, Vietnam, and Watergate—and was accepted as the framework of our foreign policy by every President from Eisenhower to [George H.W.] Bush."[249]

Texas's Cold War contributions were many, including its part in providing the nation's nuclear deterrent. The thirteen ICBMs deployed in Texas during the 1960s were part of the nation's awesome nuclear arsenal that moved Soviet leader Nikita Khrushchev to plead with President Kennedy during the October 1962 Cuban Missile Crisis to pull back from the brink and avoid civilization-ending nuclear war. Pantex was key in guaranteeing the nation's nuclear stockpile. In Lyndon Johnson, the state also provided a United States senator, vice president and president who served the nation during the most dangerous Cold War years.

Texas and Texans played key Cold War roles. As politicians, military personnel and civilians contributing to offensive preparedness, defensive preparedness and national security policy, Texans are part of the nation's Cold War legacy. With air force bases operating ICBMs and long-range bombers, Texans lived with the knowledge that the state was surely targeted by the Soviet Union and would be in the crosshairs of a nuclear attack. The Pantex Plant, the military installations that continue to operate in the state and those that do not and the former Nike sites and abandoned Atlas missile silos and converted fallout shelters across the state are all part of Texas's Cold War legacy. This legacy is worth remembering.

NOTES

Introduction

1. John F. Kennedy, "Address before the General Assembly of the United Nations, September 25, 1961," John F. Kennedy Presidential Library and Museum, accessed February 22, 2019, https://www.jfklibrary.org/archives/other-resources/john-f-kennedy-speeches/united-nations-19610925.

Chapter 1

2. Stephen E. Ambrose and Douglas G. Brinkley, *Rise to Globalism: American Foreign Policy Since 1938*, (London: Penguin Books, 2011), 53.
3. Ibid., 54–56.
4. "Churchill's Iron Curtain Speech," Westminster College, https://www.westminster-mo.edu/explore/history-traditions/IronCurtainSpeech.html.
5. Ambrose and Brinkley, *Rise to Globalism*, 76–82.
6. Ibid., 81, 83.
7. David McCullough, *Truman* (New York: Simon & Schuster, 1992), 582.
8. Ibid., 561–62.
9. Ibid., 562–63.
10. Ibid., 565, 583.

11. Ibid., 566.
12. Ambrose and Brinkley, *Rise to Globalism*, 98–99.
13. Richard Reeves, *Daring Young Men: The Heroism and Triumph of the Berlin Airlift, June 1948–May 1949* (New York: Simon & Schuster, 2010), 274.
14. Ambrose and Brinkley, *Rise to Globalism*, 101.
15. McCullough, *Truman*, 747–49.
16. Ibid., 742–44, 749.
17. Ibid., 749, 757, 761–63.
18. Ibid., 772; Ambrose and Brinkley, *Rise to Globalism*, 772.

Chapter 2

19. Evan Thomas, *Ike's Bluff: President Eisenhower's Secret Battle to Save the World* (New York: Little, Brown, 2012), 15, 112–113; Stephen E. Ambrose, *Eisenhower: Soldier and President* (New York: Simon & Schuster, 1990), 356; and John Lewis Gaddis, *The Cold War: A New History* (New York: Penguin Press, 2005), 66–67.
20. John C. Lonnquest and David F. Winkler, *To Defend and Deter: The Legacy of the United States Cold War Missile Program* (Washington, D.C.: U.S. Department of Defense, 1996), 65–66, https://atlasmissilesilo.com/Documents/AZ-D-T-999-99-ZZ-00002_ToDefendAndDeter_TheLegacyOfTheUnitedStatesColdWarMissileProgram.pdf.
21. Ibid.
22. Ibid., 209–11.
23. Ibid., 77–78.
24. Ibid., 44, 79.
25. Ibid., 220.
26. Ibid., 80–8; U.S. Army Corps of Engineers [hereafter USACE], *History of the Dyess Area Office, 18 April 1960–28 April 1962* (Los Angeles: Corps of Engineers Ballistic Missile Construction Office, 1962) 2, http://atlasmissilesilo.com/Documents/ConstructionHistory/AtlasF/578thSMS/AF-D-C-578-99-AB-00001_578thSMS_ConstructionHistory.pdf.
27. Lonnquest and Winkler, *To Defend and Deter*, 68–69, 220.
28. USACE, *Dyess Area Office*, 15–16.
29. Ibid., 16–47, 70.
30. Charles Peters, *Lyndon B. Johnson: The American Presidents* (New York: Times Books, 2010), 20.

31. USACE, *Dyess Area Office*, 16–47, 70; "Work Started on Winters Atlas Missile Site," *Winters (TX) Enterprise*, July 1, 1960, https://newspaperarchive.com/winters-enterprise-jul-01-1960-p-1/.

32. Lonnquest and Winkler, *To Defend and Deter*, 82.

33. "174-Foot Fall Kills Oplin Atlas Engineer," *Abilene (TX) Reporter-News*, April 3, 1961, https://newspaperarchive.com/abilene-reporter-news-apr-03-1961-p-1/.

34. Associated Press, "Castro Calling All Militiamen," *Abilene (TX) Reporter-News*, April 17, 1961, https://newspaperarchive.com/abilene-reporter-news-apr-17-1961-p-1/.

35. Associated Press, "Red Premier Makes Plea to Kennedy," *Abilene (TX) Reporter-News*, April 17, 1961, https://newspaperarchive.com/abilene-reporter-news-apr-18-1961-p-1/.

36. Thomas, *Ike's Bluff*, 407.

37. Ibid., 358.

38. Robert Dallek, *An Unfinished Life: John F. Kennedy, 1917–1963* (Boston: Little, Brown, 2003), 347.

39. "Special Message to Congress on Urgent National Needs," quoted in B. Wayne Blanchard, *American Civil Defense 1945–1984: The Evolution of Programs and Policies*, Monograph Series 1985, vol. 2, no. 2 (Emmitsburg, MD: National Emergency Training Center, 1986), 7–8, http://www.civildefensemuseum.com/docs/AmericanCivilDefense1945-1984.pdf.

40. "A Bow to Dyess Missile Project," *Abilene (TX) Reporter-News*, April 20, 1961; USACE, *Dyess Area Office*, document no. 16.

41. USACE, *Dyess Area Office*, 94; "96-Foot Plunge Kills Albany Site Worker," *Abilene (TX) Reporter-News*, May 9, 1961, https://newspaperarchive.com/abilene-reporter-news-may-09-1961-p-1/.

42. USACE, *Dyess Area Office*, 95; "Atlas Worker Is Electrocuted," *Abilene (TX) Reporter-News*, May 17, 1961, https://newspaperarchive.com/abilene-reporter-news-may-17-1961-p-1/.

43. Bob Phillips, "Atlas Site Given to AF: Oplin Base First Done 'On Time,'" *Abilene (TX) Reporter-News*, June 21, 1961, https://newspaperarchive.com/abilene-reporter-news-jun-21-1961-p-30/.

44. "Missile Building in Second Phase," *Abilene (TX) Reporter-News*, July 10, 1961, https://newspaperarchive.com/abilene-reporter-news-jul-10-1961-p-30/.

45. USACE, *Dyess Area Office*, 95–96; "Missile Worker in Fatal Plunge," *Abilene (TX) Reporter-News*, July 26, 1961, https://newspaperarchive.com/abilene-reporter-news-jul-26-1961-p-21/.

46. Landry Brewer, *Cold War Oklahoma* (Charleston, SC: The History Press, 2019), 26–27; "Worker Killed in 50-Foot Fall at Fargo Site," *Altus (OK) Times-Democrat*, March 24, 1961, https://news.google.com/newspapers?nid=LpWf3qrnWeoC&dat=19610324&printsec=frontpage&hl=en.

47. "McNamara Seeks Defense Money," Associated Press; Associated Press, "Kennedy Asks $3.5 Billion," *Abilene (TX) Reporter-News*, July 26, 1961, https://newspaperarchive.com/abilene-reporter-news-jul-26-1961-p-21/ ; John Lewis Gaddis, *Cold War*, 114–115.

48. Peters, *Lyndon B. Johnson*, 69.

49. USACE, *Dyess Area Office*, 98, photo no. 51; Lonnquest and Winkler, *To Defend and Deter*, 418, 553.

50. Bob Bruce, "First Atlas Missile Air-Lifted to Dyess: Secrecy Shrouds Arrival of IBM," *Abilene (TX) Reporter-News*, December 6, 1961; Associated Press, "Record Budget: Russians Enlarge Military Funds," *Abilene (TX) Reporter-News*, December 6, 1961, https://newspaperarchive.com/abilene-reporter-news-dec-06-1961-p-44/; Lonnquest and Winkler, *To Defend and Deter*, 93–94.

51. "'Lending a Hand' Saved $1-Million," *Abilene (TX) Reporter-News*, May 10, 1962, https://newspaperarchive.com/abilene-reporter-news-may-10-1962-p-48/.

52. Strategic Air Command, *SAC Missile Chronology: 1939–1988* (Offutt Air Force Base, NE: Office of the Historian, 1990), 37, http://www.siloworld.net/SAC/SAC%20Missile%20Chronology-6-4.pdf.

53. "Military Officers Quiet on Effects," *Abilene (TX) Reporter-News*, October 23, 1962, https://newspaperarchive.com/abilene-reporter-news-oct-23-1962-p-1/.

54. Peters, *Lyndon B. Johnson*, 70.

55. "'Mighty Atlas' Slated at Fair," *Abilene (TX) Reporter-News*, September 3, 1963, https://newspaperarchive.com/abilene-reporter-news-sep-03-1963-p-27/.

56. "Do-It-Yourself Silo Job Saves $6,000 at Dyess," *Abilene (TX) Reporter-News*, May 29, 1964, https://newspaperarchive.com/abilene-reporter-news-may-29-1964-p-29/.

57. Strategic Air Command, *SAC Missile Chronology*, 40, 43–44.

58. "Dyess Loses Atlas Complex: Phaseout Due by March 31," *Abilene (TX) Reporter-News*, November 19, 1964, https://newspaperarchive.com/abilene-reporter-news-nov-19-1964-p-36/.

59. "Some Missilemen to Stay at Dyess," *Abilene (TX) Reporter-News*, December 4, 1964, https://newspaperarchive.com/abilene-reporter-

news-dec-04-1964-p-45/; "Net Loss of 380 Men Due with Atlas Base Phase-Out," *Abilene (TX) Reporter-News*, December 30, 1964, https://newspaperarchive.com/abilene-reporter-news-dec-30-1964-p-6/.

60. Strategic Air Command, *SAC Missile Chronology*, 45, 47; Lonnquest and Winkler, *To Defend and Deter*, 407, 419, 553–554.
61. Bob Bruce, "Spirit of Oplin: First of 'Ready' Missiles Leaves," *Abilene (TX) Reporter-News,* January 11, 1965, https://newspaperarchive.com/abilene-reporter-news-jan-11-1965-p-13/.
62. Lonnquest and Winkler, *To Defend and Deter*, 553–54.
63. Ibid., 2–3, 29, 55, 57.
64. Ibid., 97, 99, 177, 181–82.
65. Ibid., 419–20; 555.
66. "Two Missile Bases Will Be Near Here," *Taylor (TX) Daily Press,* January 9, 1959, https://newspaperarchive.com/taylor-daily-press-jan-09-1959-p-1/.
67. Lonnquest and Winkler, *To Defend and Deter*, 420, 555.
68. "Nike Site Construction Due to Start," *Abilene (TX) Reporter-News*, August 6, 1959, https://newspaperarchive.com/abilene-reporter-news-aug-06-1959-p-6/.
69. Gayle McNutt, "Nike Men Move into First Site," *Abilene (TX) Reporter-News*, May 13, 1960, https://newspaperarchive.com/abilene-reporter-news-may-13-1960-p-62/.
70. Gayle McNutt, "High Army Brass to See Nike Tests," *Abilene (TX) Reporter-News*, May 20, 1960, https://newspaperarchive.com/abilene-reporter-news-may-20-1960-p-28/.
71. "Nike?—Atlas? Big Difference Separates Two," *Abilene (TX) Reporter-News*, May 20, 1960, https://newspaperarchive.com/abilene-reporter-news-may-20-1960-p-28/.
72. H.V. O'Brien, "Open House Planned for August," *Abilene (TX) Reporter-News,* July 7, 1960, https://newspaperarchive.com/abilene-reporter-news-jul-07-1960-p-52/.
73. H.V. O'Brien, "Army to Begin Moving in at View Nike Site Friday," *Abilene (TX) Reporter-News,* July 14, 1960, https://newspaperarchive.com/abilene-reporter-news-jul-14-1960-p-60/.
74. Bob Bruce, "10th Year for Dyess Was Big One," *Abilene (TX) Reporter-News,* January 10, 1966, https://newspaperarchive.com/abilene-reporter-news-jan-10-1966-p-27/.
75. "Army Saga of 'The Nike That Would Never Stand'; Army Missileman Sent to Viet Nam," *Abilene (TX) Reporter-News*, May 20, 1966, https://newspaperarchive.com/abilene-reporter-news-may-20-1966-p-76/.

76. "Army's 6-Year History at Dyess Closes Out June 25," *Abilene (TX) Reporter-News,* May 20, 1966, https://newspaperarchive.com/abilene-reporter-news-may-20-1966-p-77/.

77. United Press International, "Nike-Hercules Missile Sites Closed," *San Antonio (TX) Light,* August 17, 1968, https://newspaperarchive.com/san-antonio-light-aug-17-1968-p-17/.

78. Lonnquest and Winkler, *To Defend and Deter,* 419–20; 555.

79. U.S. Air Force, *The Development of Ballistic Missiles in the United States Air Force 1945–1960,* by Jacob Neufeld, 244.

80. Thomas, *Ike's Bluff,* 414.

81. "Department of State Telegram Transmitting Letter from Chairman Khrushchev to President Kennedy, October 26, 1962," John F. Kennedy Presidential Library and Museum, accessed November 5, 2019, https://microsites.jfklibrary.org/cmc/oct26/doc4.html.

82. Michael Dobbs, *One Minute to Midnight: Kennedy, Khrushchev, and Castro on the Brink of Nuclear War* (New York: Vintage Books, 2008) 98–99, 189, 386.

Chapter 3

83. B. Wayne Blanchard, *American Civil Defense 1945–1984: The Evolution of Programs and Policies,* U.S. Federal Emergency Management Agency, July 1986, 2–3. http://www.civildefensemuseum.com/docs/AmericanCivilDefense1945-1984.pdf.

84. Scott D. Hughes, "Cold War," *Encyclopedia of the Great Plains,* University of Nebraska–Lincoln, accessed October 21, 2019, http://plainshumanities.unl.edu/encyclopedia/doc/egp.war.012.

85. Ibid., 4–6; Homeland Security National Preparedness Task Force, *Civil Defense and Homeland Security: A Short History of National Preparedness Efforts,* U.S. Department of Homeland Security, September 2006, 9–10, https://training.fema.gov/hiedu/docs/dhs%20civil%20defense-hs%20-%20short%20history.pdf.

86. Blanchard, *American Civil Defense 1945–1984,* 6–7.

87. Thomas, *Ike's Bluff,* 270, 272–274.

88. Peters, *Lyndon B. Johnson,* 59, 73.

89. Thomas, *Ike's Bluff,* 274.

90. "During the Soaring '60s: National Eyes Will Be on Denton," "Not Just Cities: Rural Areas Face Woes of Fallout," "Strange New Words to

Enter Speech," *Denton (TX) Record-Chronicle*, January 31, 1960, https://newspaperarchive.com/denton-record-chronicle-jan-31-1960-p-45/.

91. "Will Organize Civil Defense Unit for North Runnels County Next Tuesday," *Winters (TX) Enterprise*, July 1, 1960, https://newspaperarchive.com/winters-enterprise-jul-01-1960-p-1/.

92. "Austin Area Likely Nuclear Bomb Target," *Daily Texan* (Austin), October 14, 1960, https://newspaperarchive.com/austin-daily-texan-oct-14-1960-p-11/.

93. Associated Press, "Khrushchev Dons Shoe, Ends Historic UN Visit," "Quemoy, Matsu Most Important Debate Issues," *Daily Texan* (Austin), October 14, 1960, https://newspaperarchive.com/austin-daily-texan-oct-14-1960-p-11/.

94. "UH to Participate in Operation Alert," *Cougar* (Houston, TX), April 27, 1961, https://newspaperarchive.com/houston-cougar-apr-27-1961-p-5/.

95. "Special Message to Congress on Urgent National Needs," quoted in B. Wayne Blanchard, *American Civil Defense 1945–1984*, 7–8.

96. Blanchard, *American Civil Defense 1945–1984*, 8.

97. James Gregory, "In the Fallout Shelter: Civil Defense in Stillwater," *Stillwater Living Magazine*, October 11, 2017, 3–4, http://stillwaterliving.com.

98. Homeland Security National Preparedness Task Force, *Civil Defense and Homeland Security*, 12.

99. "Defense System Will Be Tested," *Summer Texan* (Austin), July 7, 1961, https://newspaperarchive.com/austin-daily-texan-jul-07-1961-p-1/.

100. Stine Safety Shelter advertisement, *Amarillo (TX) Globe*, September 3, 1961, https://newspaperarchive.com/amarillo-sunday-news-globe-sep-03-1961-p-52/.

101. Morris Wilison, "Bexar Facts," *San Antonio (TX) Light*, October 9, 1961, https://newspaperarchive.com/san-antonio-light-oct-09-1961-p-15/.

102. Joe Bishop, "Historically Wrong," *San Antonio (TX) Light*, October 9, 1961, https://newspaperarchive.com/san-antonio-light-oct-09-1961-p-15/.

103. Elton Fay, Associated Press, "Military Fallout Shelters Urged by Defense Officials," *Amarillo (TX) Globe*, November 7, 1961, https://newspaperarchive.com/amarillo-globe-times-nov-07-1961-p25/.

104. Jerry Langdon, "Civil Defense Takes Close Look at Survival Chances in Amarillo," *Amarillo (TX) Daily News*, November 27, 1961, https://newspaperarchive.com/amarillo-daily-news-nov-27-1961-p-22/.

105. Gene Shelton, "Portable Hospital Exhibit," *Amarillo (TX) Daily News*, December 8, 1961, https://newspaperarchive.com/amarillo-daily-news-dec-08-1961-p-43/.

106. Elton Fay, Associated Press, "Fallout Survival Booklet to Be Distributed," *Salina (KS) Journal*, December 31, 1961, https://www.newspapers.com/image/40749006.

107. U.S. Department of Defense, Office of Civil Defense, *Family Shelter Designs*, January 1962, 2–29, http://www.civildefensemuseum.com/docs/FamilyShelterDesigns.pdf.

108. "Community Fallout Shelter Supplies—Water Storage Drums," Civil Defense Museum, 1–2, accessed April 12, 2018, http://www.civildefensemuseum.com/cdmuseum2/supply/water.html.

109. U.S. Department of Defense, Office of Civil Defense, "Fallout Shelter Food Requirements," part D, chapter 2, appendix 6 of *Federal Civil Defense Guide*, June 1964, 1–2, http://www.civildefensemuseum.com/docs/fcdg/FCDG%20Pt%20D%20Ch%202%20App%206.pdf.

110. U.S. Department of Defense. Office of Civil Defense, "Fallout Shelter Medical Kit," part D, chapter 2, appendix 8 of *Federal Civil Defense Guide*, July 1967, 1-2, http://www.civildefensemuseum.com/docs/fcdg/FCDG%20Pt%20D%20Ch%202%20App%208.pdf.

111. "Fallout Shelter Survey Shows 23 Buildings Okey," *Denton (TX) Record-Chronicle*, June 12, 1961, https://newspaperarchive.com/denton-record-chronicle-jun-12-1962-p-7/.

112. John Holt, "Missile News: Civil Defense," *Amarillo (TX) Globe-Times*, October 23, 1962, https://newspaperarchive.com/amarillo-globe-times-oct-23-1962-p-1/.

113. "Practice Sirens Quiet: 'Keep Calm,' S.A. Urged," *San Antonio (TX) Express*, October 24, 1962, https://newspaperarchive.com/san-antonio-express-oct-24-1962-p-19/.

114. John Holt, "Siren Test Cancelled: Civil Defense Interest Hiked," *Amarillo (TX) Globe-Times*, October 25, 1962, https://newspaperarchive.com/amarillo-globe-times-oct-25-1962-p-1/.

115. Ed Staats, Associated Press, "Food, Water Stockpiled: Thousands Seek Aid from Civil Defense," *Amarillo (TX) Globe-Times*, October 25, 1962, https://newspaperarchive.com/amarillo-globe-times-oct-25-1962-p-1/.

116. "In Some Stores: Canned Good Sales Up," *Denton (TX) Record-Chronicle*, October 25, 1962, https://newspaperarchive.com/denton-record-chronicle-oct-25-1962-p-11/.

117. "Here's List of What You Would Need In Way of Food," *Denton (TX) Record-Chronicle*, October 25, 1962, https://newspaperarchive.com/denton-record-chronicle-oct-25-1962-p-11/.

118. "To Be First for S.A.: Building Marked as 'Shelter,'" *San Antonio (TX) Light*, October 28, 1962, https://newspaperarchive.com/san-antonio-light-oct-28-1962-p-27/.

119. "What Would You Do in Case of Attack?" *Cougar* (Houston, TX), October 30, 1962, https://newspaperarchive.com/houston-cougar-oct-30-1962-p-2/.

120. "Better Hid Than Dead," *Daily Texan* (Austin), November 4, 1962, https://newspaperarchive.com/austin-daily-texan-nov-04-1962-p-2/.

121. Jim Clark, "School Board Considers Fallout Shelter Problems," *Amarillo (TX) Globe-Times*, November 6, 1962, https://newspaperarchive.com/amarillow-globe-times-nov-06-1962-p-2/.

122. "Civil Confusion," *Daily Texan* (Austin), December 13, 1962, https://newspaperarchive.com/austin-daily-texan-dec-13-1962-p-2/.

123. Rodney Davis, "CD Boss Defends Shelters," *Daily Texan* (Austin), December 16, 1962, https://newspaperarchive.com/austin-daily-texan-dec-16-1962-p-2/.

124. Sam Kendrick, "Eased Cuban Crisis Ends Boom in S.A. Shelter Sales," *San Antonio (TX) Express*, May 2, 1963, https://newspaperarchive.com/san-antonio-express-may-02-1963-p-7/.

125. "Civil Defense in Denton: As Tensions Ease, Citizens' Interest in Planning Lags," *Denton (TX) Record-Chronicle*, August 27, 1963, https://newspaperarchive.com/denton-record-chronicle-aug-27-1963-p-6/.

126. "First in Any Medical Facility: New Methodist Hospital Includes Fallout Shelters," *San Antonio (TX) Express/News*, September 22, 1963, https://newspaperarchive.com/san-antonio-express-and-news-sep-22-1963-p-85/.

127. "Civil Defense Sets Training Program," *Cougar* (Houston, TX), November 8, 1963, https://newspaperarchive.com/houston-cougar-nov-08-1963-p-12/.

128. Judy Downs, "In Civil Defense Project: Professors Try Shelter Living," *Daily Texan* (Austin), December 6, 1963, https://newspaperarchive.com/austin-daily-texan-dec-06-1963-p-3/.

129. "Denton: New CD Program Underway," *Denton (TX) Record-Chronicle*, December 23, 1963, https://newspaperarchive.com/denton-record-chronicle-dec-23-1963-p-10/.

130. Mike Engleman, "Taking a Word-Tour of the New Underground Center," *Denton (TX) Record-Chronicle*, February 16, 1964, https://newspaperarchive.com/denton-record-chronicle-feb-16-1964-p-22/.
131. Ibid.
132. "Texas Underground School Praised," *Denton (TX) Record-Chronicle*, February 16, 1964, https://newspaperarchive.com/denton-record-chronicle-feb-16-1964-p-22/.
133. Bill Lee, "Civil Defense: Apathy of American Public Worries Many U.S. Officials," *San Antonio (TX) Light*, January 31, 1965, https://newspaperarchive.com/san-antonio-light-jan-31-1965-p-8/.
134. "Courthouse Praised for Fallout Shelter," *Amarillo (TX) Globe-Times*, June 17, 1965, https://newspaperarchive.com/amarillo-globe-times-jun-17-1965-p-35/.
135. "Rotary Club Hears Speech on Shelters," *Denton (TX) Record-Chronicle*, February 4, 1966, https://newspaperarchive.com/denton-record-chronicle-feb-04-1966-p-3/.
136. "Area Groups Learn Fallout Shelter Design," *Cougar* (Houston, TX), March 10, 1966, https://newspaperarchive.com/houston-daily-cougar-mar-10-1966-p-10/.
137. Julian Rodriguez, "More Than 100 Residents Participate in Shelter Exercise During 'Air Attack,'" *San Antonio (TX) Express*, June 17, 1966, https://newspaperarchive.com/san-antonio-express-jun-17-1966-p-14/.
138. "City Council Announces Tower Voice Contract," *Daily Texan* (Austin), November 18, 1966, https://newspaperarchive.com/austin-daily-texan-nov-18-1966-p-1/.
139. "'Voices' to Boom in Morning Test," *Daily Texan* (Austin), December 2, 1966, https://newspaperarchive.com/austin-daily-texan-dec-02-1966-p-1/.
140. Blanchard, *American Civil Defense 1945–1984*; Homeland Security National Preparedness Task Force, *Civil Defense and Homeland Security*, 13–14.

Chapter 4

141. Ross Phares and Paul O. Cormier, "Amarillo Air Force Base," in *Handbook of Texas*, Texas State Historical Association, published 1976, updated November 1, 1994, https://www.tshaonline.org/handbook/entries/amarillo-air-force-base.

142. David Minor, "Sheppard Air Force Base," in *Handbook of Texas*, Texas State Historical Association, published 1976, updated June 1, 1995, https://www.tshaonline.org/handbook/entries/sheppard-air-force-base.

143. Ibid.

144. Ibid.

145. Glenn Hegar, "Sheppard Air Force Base: Economic Impact on the Texas Economy, 2019," comptroller.texas.gov, accessed January 4, 2022, https://comptroller.texas.gov/economy/economic-data/military/sheppard.php.

146. Art Leatherwood, "Dyess Air Force Base," in *Handbook of Texas*, Texas State Historical Association, published 1976, updated September 5, 2019, https://www.tshaonline.org/handbook/entries/dyess-air-force-base.

147. Ibid.

148. Ibid.

149. Glenn Hegar, "Dyess Air Force Base: Economic Impact on the Texas Economy, 2019," comptroller.texas.gov, accessed January 4, 2022, https://comptroller.texas.gov/economy/economic-data/military/dyess.php.

150. Sangeeta Singg and William A. Allen, "Goodfellow Air Force Base," in *Handbook of Texas*, Texas State Historical Association, published 1976, updated October 1, 1995, https://www.tshaonline.org/handbook/entries/goodfellow-air-force-base.

151. Ibid.

152. Glenn Hegar, "Goodfellow Air Force Base: Economic Impact on the Texas Economy, 2019," comptroller.texas.gov, accessed January 4, 2022, https://comptroller.texas.gov/economy/economic-data/military/goodfellow.php.

153. Timothy M. Brown and Lane Bourgeois, "Randolph Air Force Base," in *Handbook of Texas*, Texas State Historical Association, published 1976, updated February 13, 2018, https://www.tshaonline.org/handbook/entries/randolph-air-force-base.

154. Ibid.

155. Ibid.

156. Art Leatherwood and J.T.L. English, "Lackland Air Force Base," in *Handbook of Texas*, Texas State Historical Association, published 1976, updated March 14, 2018, https://www.tshaonline.org/handbook/entries/lackland-air-force-base.

157. Ibid.

158. Ibid.
159. Art Leatherwood and Laurie E. Jasinski, "Kelly Air Force Base," in *Handbook of Texas*, Texas State Historical Association, published 1976, updated April 4, 2018, https://www.tshaonline.org/handbook/entries/kelly-air-force-base.
160. Ibid.
161. Glenn Hegar, "Port of Entry: Port San Antonio: Impact to the Texas Economy, 2019," comptroller.texas.gov, accessed January 5, 2022, https://comptroller.texas.gov/economy/economic-data/ports/port-san-antonio.php#:~:text=The%20Comptroller%20estimates%20that%20the,in%202018%20(Exhibit%204).
162. Art Leatherwood, "Laughlin Air Force Base," in *Handbook of Texas*, Texas State Historical Association, published 1976, updated March 1, 1995, https://www.tshaonline.org/handbook/entries/laughlin-air-force-base.
163. Glenn Hegar, "Laughlin Air Force Base: Impact to the Texas Economy, 2019," comptroller.texas.gov, accessed January 5, 2022, https://comptroller.texas.gov/economy/economic-data/military/laughlin.php.
164. Steven G. Gamble and Ruedele Turner, "Reese Air Force Base," in *Handbook of Texas*, Texas State Historical Association, published 1976, updated January 1, 1996, https://www.tshaonline.org/handbook/entries/reese-air-force-base.
165. Art Leatherwood, "James Connally Air Force Base," in *Handbook of Texas*, Texas State Historical Association, published 1976, updated April 25, 2019, https://www.tshaonline.org/handbook/entries/james-connally-air-force-base.
166. Art Leatherwood, "Bergstrom Air Force Base," in *Handbook of Texas*, Texas State Historical Association, published 1976, updated November 1, 1994, https://www.tshaonline.org/handbook/entries/bergstrom-air-force-base.
167. John Manguso, "Fort Sam Houston," in *Handbook of Texas*, Texas State Historical Association, published 1976, updated May 16, 2018, https://www.tshaonline.org/handbook/entries/fort-sam-houston.
168. Ibid.
169. Ibid.
170. Ibid.
171. Glenn Hegar, "Joint Base San Antonio: Economic Impact on the Texas Economy, 2019," comptroller.texas.gov, accessed January 5, 2022, https://comptroller.texas.gov/economy/economic-data/military/jbsa.php.

172. Leon C. Metz, "Fort Bliss," in *Handbook of Texas*, Texas State Historical Association, published 1976, updated October 3, 2019, https://www.tshaonline.org/handbook/entries/fort-bliss.

173. Ibid.

174. Ibid.

175. Glenn Hegar, "Fort Bliss: Economic Impact on the Texas Economy, 2019," comptroller.texas.gov, accessed January 5, 2022, https://comptroller.texas.gov/economy/economic-data/military/fort-bliss.php.

176. Frederick L. Briuer, "Fort Hood," in *Handbook of Texas*, Texas State Historical Association, published 1976, updated January 27, 2018, https://www.tshaonline.org/handbook/entries/fort-hood.

177. Ibid.

178. Glenn Hegar, "Fort Hood: Economic Impact on the Texas Economy, 2019," comptroller.texas.gov, accessed January 5, 2022, https://comptroller.texas.gov/economy/economic-data/military/fort-hood.php.

179. Art Leatherwood, "Naval Air Station, Corpus Christi," in *Handbook of Texas*, Texas State Historical Association, published 1976, updated December 1, 1995, https://www.tshaonline.org/handbook/entries/naval-air-station-corpus-christi.

180. Ibid.

181. Glenn Hegar, "Naval Air Station Corpus Christi: Economic Impact on the Texas Economy, 2019," comptroller.texas.gov, accessed January 5, 2022, https://comptroller.texas.gov/economy/economic-data/military/nas-corpus.php.

182. Art Leatherwood, "Naval Air Station, Dallas," in *Handbook of Texas*, Texas State Historical Association, published 1976, updated November 1, 1995, https://www.tshaonline.org/handbook/entries/naval-air-station-dallas.

183. Ibid.

184. "Naval Air Station, Kingsville," *Handbook of Texas*, Texas State Historical Association, published 1976, updated May 1, 1995, https://www.tshaonline.org/handbook/entries/naval-air-station-kingsville.

185. Glenn Hegar, "Naval Air Station Kingsville: Economic Impact on the Texas Economy, 2019," comptroller.texas.gov, accessed January 6, 2022, https://comptroller.texas.gov/economy/economic-data/military/nas-kingsville.php.

186. Art Leatherwood, "Naval Air Station Joint Reserve Base Fort Worth," in *Handbook of Texas*, Texas State Historical Association, published 1976, updated November 15, 2013, https://www.tshaonline.org/handbook/entries/naval-air-station-joint-reserve-base-fort-worth.

187. Glenn Hegar, "Naval Air Station Joint Reserve Base Fort Worth: Economic Impact on the Texas Economy, 2019, comptroller.texas.gov, accessed January 6, 2022, https://comptroller.texas.gov/economy/economic-data/military/nas-fortworth.php#:~:text=Naval%20Air%20Station%20Joint%20Reserve%20Base%20Fort%20Worth%20Economic%20Impact,the%20Texas%20economy%20in%202019.

188. Christopher Long, "Red River Army Depot," in *Handbook of Texas*, Texas State Historical Association, published 1976, updated August 4, 2020, https://www.tshaonline.org/handbook/entries/red-river-army-depot.

189. Glenn Hegar, "Red River Army Depot: Economic Impact on the Texas Economy, 2019," comptroller.texas.gov, accessed January 6, 2022, https://comptroller.texas.gov/economy/economic-data/military/red-river.php.

Chapter 5

190. "History," U.S. Department of Energy, https://pantex.energy.gov/about/history; H. Allen Anderson and Laurie E. Jasinski, "Pantex," in *Handbook of Texas*, Texas State Historical Association, published 1976, updated August 12, 2008, https://www.tshaonline.org/handbook/entries/pantex.

191. "History," U.S. Department of Energy; Anderson and Jasinski, "Pantex."

192. Brianna Nofil, "The Secret 'White Trains' That Carried Nuclear Weapons around the U.S.," *HISTORY*, May 26, 2021, https://www.history.com/news/nuclear-transportation-u-s-white-trains-cold-war?cmpid=email-hist-mysterious-2021-0507-05072021&om_rid=&~campaign=hist-mysterious-2021-0507.

193. Ibid.

194. Ibid.

195. Kenneth A. Briggs, "Religious Leaders Objecting to Nuclear Arms," *New York Times*, September 8, 1981, https://www.nytimes.com/1981/09/08/us/religious-leaders-objecting-to-nuclear-arms.html.

196. Associated Press, "Relatives of 3 Killed in Blast at Nuclear Plant Lose Suit," *New York Times*, October 3, 1981, https://www.nytimes.com/1981/10/03/us/relatives-of-3-killed-in-blast-at-nuclear-plant-lose-suit.html.

197. "About the Peace Farm," Peace Farm, http://www.peacefarm.us/about.htm.

198. Anderson and Jasinski, "Pantex."

199. Ibid.

200. Ibid.

201. "Pantex Contracting Brings Positive Economic Impact to Local Businesses," KFDA, November 30, 2016, https://www.newschannel10.com/story/33831614/pantex-contracting-brings-positive-economic-impact-to-local-businesses/.

Chapter 6

202. Don S. Kirschner, *Cold War Exile: The Unclosed Case of Maurice Halperin* (Columbia: University of Missouri Press, 1995), 17, 19–21.

203. Ibid., 23–24, 32.

204. Ibid., 36–37.

205. Ibid., 39.

206. Ibid., 39–40.

207. Ibid., 41–42.

208. Ibid., 49–55.

209. Ibid., 57.

210. George Lynn Cross, *Professors, Presidents & Politicians: Civil Rights and the University of Oklahoma, 1890–1968* (Norman, OK: University of Oklahoma Press, 1981), 112; Eric Eugene Beau, "Leon Phillips and the New Deal in Oklahoma" (master's thesis, University of Central Oklahoma, 2015), 46–47, 49.

211. Beau, "Leon Phillips," 66.

212. Cross, *Professors, Presidents & Politicians*, 124.

213. Kirschner, *Cold War Exile*, 60–61; Wayne A. Wiegand and Shirley A. Wiegand, "Sooner State Civil Liberties in Perilous Times, 1940–1941, Part 2: Oklahoma's Little Dies Committee," *Chronicles of Oklahoma* 85, no. 1 (Spring 2007): 23, 25.

214. Beau, "Leon Phillips," 69.

215. Ibid., 70–71.

216. Kirschner, *Cold War Exile*, 112–16.

217. Katie Marton, *True Believer: Stalin's Last American Spy* (New York: Simon & Schuster, 2016), 50, 72.

218. Ibid., 114.

219. Ibid., 42–43, 50.

220. Kirschner, *Cold War Exile*, 112–16.

221. Ibid., 130–31.
222. Ibid., 133.
223. Ibid., 134–35, 137–40.
224. Ibid., 277.
225. Ibid.
226. Ibid., 278–79.
227. Ibid., 279–80.
228. Ibid., 280–81.
229. Ibid., 281–82, 302.
230. Ibid., 282.
231. Ibid., 290–92.
232. Ibid., 314.
233. Ibid., 315–16.
234. John Earl Haynes and Harvey Klehr, *Venona: Decoding Soviet Espionage in America* (New Haven, CT: Yale University Press, 1999), 6, 8–10.
235. Ibid., 101–2.
236. Ibid.
237. Ibid., 102–3.
238. Allen Weinstein and Alexander Vassiliev, *The Haunted Wood: Soviet Espionage in America—The Stalin Era* (New York: Random House, 1999), xxiii, 106, 256.
239. Haynes and Klehr, *Venona*, 9–11, 15–16, 35–36, 90, 129–30, 160–61, 163, 170–73, 220, 223–4, 307–11, 331–32.

Chapter 7

240. Hughes, "Cold War."
241. Ibid.
242. "U.S. Military Fatal Casualties of the Korean War for Home-State-of-Record: Texas," National Archives, accessed December 26, 2021, https://www.archives.gov/files/research/military/korean-war/casualty-lists/tx-alpha.pdf.
243. Ibid.
244. "General MacArthur's Farewell Speech—Duty, Honor, Country (May 12, 1962)," Jackson State University, http://www.jsums.edu/arotc/duty-honor-country/.
245. Hughes, "Cold War."

246. Colleen Kane, "7 Doomsday Bunkers for Surviving the Apocalypse, No Matter Your Budget," *Money*, accessed April 7, 2022, https://money.com/doomsday-bunkers-survive-apocalypse-sale/.

247. Mary K. Jacob, "Missile Silo Designed to Withstand Nuclear Strike on Sale for $380K," *New York Post*, January 31, 2022, https://nypost.com/2022/01/31/missile-silo-designed-to-withstand-nuclear-strike-on-sale-for-380k/.

248. Hughes, "Cold War."

249. Clark Clifford and Richard Holbrooke, *Counsel to the President: A Memoir* (New York: Random House, 1991), 660.

ABOUT THE AUTHOR

Landry Brewer is Bernhardt Assistant Professor of History for Southwestern Oklahoma State University and teaches at the Sayre campus. Brewer is also the author of *Cold War Oklahoma* and *Cold War Kansas*, and since 2006, he has cohosted a morning talk show on KECO Radio in Elk City, Oklahoma, with his twin brother, Nathan.

Brewer and his wife, Erin, have five children and live in Elk City.

Visit us at
www.historypress.com
·······································